A Psychiatrist's Guide: Helping Parents Reach Their Depressed Tween

GAYANI DeSILVA, MD

ISBN-13: 9780988585539
BISAC CODES:
FAM003000 (FAMILY & RELATIONSHIPS / Adolescence)
PSY005000 (PSYCHOLOGY & PSYCHIATRY / Child Psychiatry)
PSY006000 (PSYCHOLOGY & PSYCHIATRY / Child Psychology)

Nationwide Distribution through Ingram & New Leaf Distributing Company.

TVGuestpert Publishing and the TVG logo are trademarks of Jacquie Jordan Inc.

TVGuestpert & TVGuestpert Publishing are subsidiaries of Jacquie Jordan Inc.

TVGuestpert & TVGuestpert Publishing are visionary media companies that seek to educate, enlighten, and entertain the masses with the highest level of integrity. Our full service production company, publishing house, management, and media development firm promise to engage you creatively and honor you and ourselves, as well as the community, in order to bring about fulfillment and abundance both personally and professionally.

Front Book Cover Design by Jonathan Fong
Book Design by Carole Allen Design Studio
Author Headshots by Starla Fortunato
Copy Edited by Madeline Fitzgerald
Edited by TVGuestpert Publishing
Stock Photo by iStock
Published by TVGuestpert Publishing

11664 National Blvd, #345
Los Angeles, CA. 90064
310-584-1504
www.TVGPublishing.com
www.TVGuestpert.com
First Printing May 9th, 2017
10 9 8 7 6 5 4 3 2 1

A Psychiatrist's Guide: Helping Parents Reach Their Depressed Tween

GAYANI DeSILVA, MD

TO:

My patients,

My son, Henry Nalin Reynolds,

and

My parents, Himasiri and Constance DeSilva

ACKNOWLEDGMENTS

The people who provided the inspiration for this book cannot be named here. It is my patients who gave me the inspiration to write this book and the stories that make this information come alive. I acknowledge every parent who reached out to me, and professionals like me, in the effort to understand and help their children. My mentor, collaborator, and overall beautiful human being, Vickie Falcone, helped me develop both as a writer and keen observer of the parents I serve. I thank Jacquie Jordan for just about everything, most importantly for believing in my vision and me. My friends and family, notably Constance DeSilva, MD; Himasiri DeSilva, MD; Shailesh Bambardekar, Anastacia Escoboza; Darcia Dexter; Mark Bravo, DN, JD; Anne Marie D'Agostino; Gloria Cardones; Julie Ryu, MD; Rosemarie Fleming, LCSW; Wayne Lenz, LMFT; and Alec Shirzadi, DO, for their expertise, encouragement, unconditional kindness, and babysitting, which provided me the much-needed space to stop, think, and write. To George Korich; Heather Blackmore; Clara Cantorna; Yolanda Gabrielle, LCSW; Bob Barbosa; Adam Kline; Mike Lebeau, JD; Betty Reynolds; Karen Medley, RN; Bob Bailey, MD; Lex Grapentine, MD; Andrew Sassani, MD; George Davis, MD; Carol Larroque, MD; Jeanne Bereiter, MD; David Mullen, MD; Sarah Bennett-Reaves, PhD; Jeanne Burns Leary, MD; and Jevelyn Yonchar, MD, who nurtured the writer, mother, and healer within me. Edward Gibson, through the collaborative process of glassblowing, sparked the courage to commit to writing this book.

I am grateful to Laguna Family Health Center, Inc.; Holly Viloria, NP; Katelyn Hicks; and Kerry Johnson for creating a work environment that is ideal for growth, creativity, and profound healing. Behind the scenes, Stephanie Cobian has been my advocate and friend. Jayne Shane for helping me advocate for children and mental illness care. Kriz Crane for making this world and me more beautiful. Starla Fortunato for drawing out the fire and passion within.

No page would have been written without the continual kindness, generosity, and love of my son, Henry. He helped me solve technical challenges, actively listened to all my musings, offered insight about how to reach children, and provided unlimited hugs. Henry is the reason for my smile and the impetus for this book; at only nine years old, he said, "Mommy, help the parents, and the kids will heal."

Being an engaged parent inspired me to realize my personal goals and meet them. It is not just a labor of love to raise a child, it is a mutual experience of creating abundance and joy. I am grateful to be a mother and a physician, and blessed by the opportunity to touch the lives of my patients, their families, and my readers.

A Psychiatrist's Guide:
HELPING PARENTS REACH THEIR DEPRESSED TWEEN

CONTENTS

Foreword

It was the summer before I was to start eighth grade when my parents drove my brother four hours to the big city to meet with a "special" doctor. The trip was shrouded in shame and secrecy. For years, I had watched from the sidelines as my parents struggled to both connect with and discipline my brother. Nothing they did seemed to work. They tried yelling, lecturing, ignoring, grounding, reasoning with, punishing, and more lecturing. It was painful to watch—and powerfully ineffective.

After a battery of tests, they returned home with a diagnosis that would rock my family to its core, and strip me of any sense of a "normal" childhood, something any middle schooler will tell you is all they want.

My mother was the calmest, kindest, and most patient human I have ever known. She was the picture of Southern gentility and grace. But the next day, after returning from their trip to the big city, after what seemed like hours of her pleading, begging, and otherwise trying to reach my brother, she finally lost it. I had never before seen my mother yell or even raise her voice. But now this former picture of poise was screaming at the top of her lungs. It wouldn't be the last time. My parents continued to live at the proverbial end of their rope for years.

I now realize that both of my parents fell into the unhelpful parenting patterns that Dr. DeSilva calls Fix-It Parenting. One parent was strict and unrelenting (harsh boundaries). The other compensated by giving in (no boundaries). Ultimately, both proved damaging. Though my parents meant well, and loved my brother very much, they had no tools for redirecting my brother's behaviors…or reaching him. Where would they have learned them? There were no books, support groups, or blogs on this topic, and it seemed they learned very little from the treating professionals. It was the 1970s and the mentality at that time was *drop your kid off at the door of the shrink's office and pick him up when he's done.*

My brother's life path landed him in drug and alcohol rehab when he was in his twenties. At the time, I was seven months pregnant with my first child. To assist in his healing, my parents and I participated in an intensive and highly emotional forty-hour family week program with my brother. It was during that family week that I first learned about the parenting practices that had done the most damage in our family, and those that healed. Our family, it seemed, had a lot to "un-learn."

Family week had a profound impact on me. While there, I made a promise to myself that would change the trajectory of my personal and professional life. I vowed to myself, and my unborn child, that I would do everything in my power to end the cycle of dysfunction and poor communication in my family. This promise set me on a twenty-four-year path as a parenting speaker, author, and coach. I have made my living learning and teaching parents positive skills for interacting with their children.

When Dr. DeSilva asked me to help with *A Psychiatrist's Guide: Helping Parents Reach Their Depressed Tween*, I was both honored and motivated to be part of a book that would have so helped *my* family in their time of need. Dr. DeSilva is a teacher first and a physician second. She will tell you that one of her greatest strengths is her passion for educating parents about what really works to heal their anxious or depressed child. As a result, *A Psychiatrist's Guide* reads more like comforting kitchen table wisdom than the work of a Harvard-trained psychiatrist.

With a combination of compassion, wisdom, and hope, Dr. DeSilva teaches parenting skills that work to meet the needs of children struggling with anxiety or depression. She offers up advice that is both research-backed and accessible. Her heartfelt intention is to help parents take back their power and understand that even though they will be working with experts, they will always be the most important expert in their child's life. She views the treatment process as highly collaborative and shows parents how to best partner with their child's treatment team...while simultaneously understanding the tremendous influence they have over their children.

Any parent will tell you that raising a preteen is challenging enough without the additional suffering that comes with managing anxiety or depression. "Overwhelming" is too kind a word. Fortunately for you, a caring, wise guide has spent her life honing the skills that can mean the difference between suffering and sanity in your family. In *A Psychiatrist's Guide: Helping Parents Reach Their Depressed Tween*, Dr. DeSilva has opened up her toolbox, and her heart, and created nothing less than a work of healing art.

Vickie Falcone, MA
Author of *Buddha Never Raised Kids & Jesus Didn't Drive Carpool*
Conscious Relationship Coach, Speaker
Los Angeles, California

Introduction

Nothing is more important to a parent than the wellbeing of their child. Raising a child who struggles with depression and anxiety leaves many parents feeling scared and helpless. This is how most parents feel when they walk into my office. They have reached the end of their rope and feel desperate for help. If that's not enough, in this state of desperation, parents then have to share the most vulnerable parts of themselves with me. When parents are open to learning and applying my "ten tools of the trade," their children benefit and the healing process is amplified.

Ten-year-old Michael and his mother sat across from me. Michael fidgeted with the book on his lap, flipping it open, closed, and open again. His mother sat rigid on the edge of her chair nervously bouncing her foot. Michael struggled with anxiety and depression. Michael, like many kids with these diagnoses, was intelligent and at the same time unable to concentrate and acted like he wanted to be left alone.

Though he had a good response to the antidepressant medication, he continued to have moments of being withdrawn and irritable. What remained was Michael's strained relationship with his parents. When his parents made a request of Michael, like asking him to practice his clarinet, unload the dishwasher, or get dressed, he dug his feet in. His parents complained that they had trouble orchestrating even the simplest of tasks. His mother shared that she would eventually get very frustrated and resort to demands like "go practice your clarinet now," even though she admitted that her demands rarely invited cooperation.

She turned to me and asked, "What do I do in those moments? He gets so irritable and focused on other things."

She felt discouraged and concerned.

I taught Michael's mom how to have a conversation with him.

I started by asking Michael, "What is it like for you to be ordered to do something like practice the clarinet?"

I went on to ask him a number of open-ended questions. I asked what it was like for him when faced with choosing between the things he wants to do versus things his parents want him to do (that he doesn't want to do). I inquired about what his parents' demands feel like for him. I asked him what kind of relationship he wanted to have with his mom.

I inquired, "Are there times that your mom asks you to do things when you are busy doing something else?"

I asked him what he would rather be doing.

"I would rather read or play games," he answered.

I continued, "Do you think you can make a choice about that?"

He replied, "I don't know."

I went on to explain. "In those moments, you actually can make a choice. When you are focusing on something and it gets taken away from what you first wanted to do, you can choose to just do the new thing, and also choose to come back to the first thing you were doing. You can actually tell your mind, *I see that game but I'm going to put the clarinet first.*"

Michael took my words in as he looked through the pages of the book on his lap. Each time he did, I would gently offer, "I know the book is interesting, isn't it? It's hard to take your eyes off the book. Do you think you could close the book for me and I promise, after we are done talking, you can get right back to your book?"

Mom watched as he chose to pay attention to me without my having to use directives. She watched him fully engage in the conversation. It was clear he was trying to do what was asked of him. I watched her relax back into her chair and stop bouncing her feet. All the lines in her face seemed to melt. She looked much more at peace.

She said, "That all sounds so nice. I can see how that would be helpful but I don't know how to do that."

As a psychiatrist, I work with tweens—the precious age of ten to thirteen—with mental illness, which includes anxiety and depression, an often-genetic condition. My devoted career has schooled me in the delicate parenting skills that are required to handle such a child.

She continued, "I've read everything out there about anxiety and depression but nothing tells me what to say to my child."

The ability to communicate rather than direct the child is one of the most important gifts I can bestow a parent.

I whole-heartedly offered, "I will write a book."

To which she insisted, "Yes, you should write that book."

You now hold in your hands the book that Michael's mother, and many parents, asked for over the years…the guide for how to help heal and connect with a child struggling with anxiety and depression.

This book is for you if you've asked yourself any of the following questions:

"Does my child have anxiety and depression?"

"Did I do something to cause it?"

"What do I do?"

"What is going on inside my child's head?"

"How can I help my child feel better?"

"Am I doing the right thing?"

"Is this just a phase that my child will grow out of?"

"Am I making too much out of his moodiness?"

"Should we start medication?"

"Is this the best treatment?"

"What is the best way to help my child through depression or anxiety?"

"What's the best way to parent my depressed/anxious child?"

"How do I choose between all these choices and all the information out there?"
"Who do I trust?"
"Who is the best therapist for my child?"
"What is the difference between a therapist and a psychiatrist? Does my child need both?"
"How do I know if therapy is working?"
"When will my child start to feel better?"
"I feel like I've lost my child… When will I get my child back?"
"Am I a bad parent?"

In the first few months of parenting a newborn, as new parents we ask ourselves, "What do I do with this baby?" We then read as much as we can about those first weeks and months and/or talk to friends and family in order to learn how to be a good parent. After a few years, our confidence in our parenting increases and our child heads off to school. That transition pulls us out of our old comfort zone and brings new challenges that require us to adjust our parenting to meet the emerging needs of our child. This cycle of moving from "not knowing" to "knowing" how to meet new parenting challenges happens throughout the life of our child.

Most parents first receive a diagnosis of anxiety or depression from a school counselor, pediatrician, or family doctor. The first thing parents feel is panic. They are immediately thrust out of their comfort zone. They don't know what to do or how to handle things and they now have to rely on other people to help them. This time it's not just friends and family. Parents now have to place their faith in members of the child's treatment team, strangers. That places parents in a position of vulnerability. When the wrench of anxiety or depression is thrown into the mix of parenting, everything changes. At this point, parents don't know what to do and they fear doing the wrong thing, but they often don't know the right thing to do. This can cause even the most secure parent to feel ignorant and out of control. Parents feel scared, nervous, sad, disappointed, and frustrated. Sadly, up until now, there hasn't been a lot of support for parents about how to specifically help their child navigate anxiety or depression. There is plenty of information available about mental illness, but few sources for how to relate to—and even heal—your child.

My path of working with parents started long before I became a psychiatrist but rather accidentally in the pediatric ICU during med school. While working in the PICU, I saw parents endure intense pain and suffering as their children were subjected to incredibly invasive and painful procedures. Watching the intense pain and fear these parents were going through struck a deep chord with me. From that point, I was called to reach out and support these parents. I used to sit with parents for hours and simply listen to them. It is a terrifying experience when a child is suffering and we can't do anything about it. I found it comforting that I could make a small positive difference. My cohorts eventually started referring to me as the "Parent Whisperer." I was just following my passion.

Twenty-three years later, I am still passionate about supporting parents in their time of greatest need. Still today, I first listen for the story, not the problem. From that vantage point, I identify the tangible problems we need to solve. When I am treating a child, I focus on the whole family and the total experience of being a parent. As a parent of a young child myself, I bring a deep understanding of the joys and challenges of parenting. I understand and help parents be gentle with themselves, as I remind them that raising children who are anxious or depressed need not be a perfect endeavor. It's up and down. There are plenty of opportunities to make mistakes. I help parents reframe their mistakes as simply "things that aren't going the way we want them to go." With this mindset, so much healing is possible.

Parenting a child with depression or anxiety feels especially challenging and confusing because it's hard to relate or connect to someone who is afflicted. I understand this obstacle and thrive on helping parents dissolve the barriers so they can make a meaningful connection with their child.

Though it may seem impossible right now, you can learn ways to connect with your anxious or depressed child and feel more confident as a parent. When parents first learn about their child's diagnosis, the first thing that happens is they now have to rely on their therapist and psychiatrist for supporting guidance. This sets up a tangible power differential. All of a sudden parents feel helpless. They don't know how to help their child and have to rely on other people to reach their child. *It is my intention in this book to help you reclaim your power and confidence; to help you understand that you are still the most important person in your child's life; and to help you know that you can help your child as much as (if not more than) their therapist and psychiatrist.* This happens once parents are empowered with tools that work to connect with their child and therefore catalyze the healing process. Though not widely available, these skills are simple to learn, understand, and implement. I know, I've seen thousands of my patients do it. You can too. If you provide the willingness, I will provide the information.

CHAPTER 1

Mental Illness

Most parents are well equipped to help their children soothe themselves and feel better when it comes to the usual worries and nervousness of growing up. When there is an anxiety disorder brewing the usual parenting skills are not wholly effective, and parents are left feeling like their skills are inadequate or incorrect. This is not due to inadequate parenting, but to the nature of their child's psychiatric condition, including panic disorder, social anxiety disorder, or depression.

Mental disorders have a biological origin. The symptoms of anxiety and depression arise because of a chemical issue in the brain. Unhealthy neural pathways lead to troublesome behaviors like panic attacks, irritability, low motivation, and crying spells. While these behaviors can be triggered by events and psychological reactions to situations and feelings, the symptoms are ultimately driven by biology. For parents to effectively help their child struggling with anxiety or depression, they must incorporate a biological intervention as well as psychological techniques. Even parents who generally felt good about their parenting skills can lose their confidence in the face of a child diagnosed with a mental illness.

Sean and his father sat on my couch as I started my assessment. When I asked Sean if he knew why he was there to see me, he shrugged his shoulders, smirked, and said, "I don't know."

His father told me that he has seen his son become increasingly more anxious over the previous several months. Earlier that week, his son had had several panic attacks.

"I don't understand, we are so close and I would do anything for him. But he gets so worked up with anxiety that I can't reach him."

He went on, "I don't know how to help him. It doesn't seem like logic works, and I don't understand what he is so worried about. He hasn't been able to go to school at all this week."

Sean's father clearly felt close to his son and was concerned. Watching Sean, at just ten years old, struggle through panic attacks every day, Sean's father felt helpless.

For Sean, we created a treatment plan that included individual therapy once a week and support for Sean's parents. His parents learned to support him. Therapy helped him learn coping mechanisms to use whenever he started to feel anxious or scared. Prescribed medications diminished the acuteness of Sean's panic attacks. His parents learned how to partner with the school to reduce the sources of anxiety, such as implementing less homework, more time to complete tasks and tests, and assisting with social situations. Within a few months, Sean's panic attacks stopped, and he was able to accept help whenever his parents reached out to support him.

Mental illnesses, such as anxiety and depressive disorders, arise due to genes that drive neurons to react in certain ways when confronted by psychological and situational challenges, or even to initiate a depressive or anxious episode out of the blue. A child whose brain has the genes for depression is not able to generate enough neurotransmitters, like serotonin, to handle a significant stressor, like the loss of a loved one. This combination of brain chemistry and stressor can plummet the child into a depressive episode. Without the genes for depression, a child may get sad when confronted by a loss, but not experience a depressive episode. That means, parents cannot cause a depressive or anxiety disorder in their children. One caveat to this statement is in the case of abuse, which changes the way the brain reacts and can cause the development of severe anxiety and depressive disorders, and other mental illness, in tweens. Most parents, however, can let themselves off the hook by understanding that biology is the culprit.

Parents want to please their child. Parents typically feel miserable when their child feels miserable. Most parents strongly empathize with what their child is feeling and want their children to be happy. The parents of my tween patients tell me repeatedly, "I just want him to be happy. He is such a great kid." However, children cannot be happy all the time. When children are stuck in a depressed mood for a prolonged time, parents begin to worry...a lot. When parents can understand and learn how to validate their child's experience and accept that the child is depressed, it takes away the pressure they feel to fix it. It's a very powerful thing to do. It's very hard for most parents to just accept that their child is feeling badly...to simply sit and share that feeling with them.

Parents are trained from pregnancy to care for their child's every need. In parenting healthy children, you can't provide for every need—more so when your child is depressed or anxious. It's just not possible, so some acceptance around this truth can go a long way toward a parent's peace of mind. Parents benefit their children the most when they learn skills, like validating experiences. This helps them live and thrive with the depression and anxiety disorders, and start the process of healing, which often takes considerable time.

Before we set forth to interact with a child, we must take care of ourselves first. We must look at our mood state—our feelings, our anxiety, and our wishes—before we initiate a connection with our child. This includes validating our feelings and experiences. If we can't validate our feelings and experiences, then how are we supposed to effectively validate another being's feelings and experiences?

I am often confronted with the behavior of parents when they direct their child to discuss an incident during the week when the child misbehaved. Anitra, a nine-year-old girl, struggled with oppositional and defiant behavior with her parents. She was diagnosed with a disruptive mood dysregulation disorder. Her disorder led her to behaviors that were disruptive to her life, such as depression, mood swings, anger, rage episodes, increased anxiety, and loss of physical control. Though her parents tried to make a positive statement before telling me about their behavioral challenges during the week, Anitra would storm out of the room. Anitra's parents told me that they "can't talk with Anitra about her behaviors" because she becomes angry, shuts down, or stomps out of the room. Their good efforts at using positive statements before negative statements were not working for their child. Instead of increasing understanding and cooperative behaviors, it fueled the distance between them and the escalation of her out-of-control behaviors. They continually directed Anitra to confess her poor behavior to me.

With Anitra in the playroom, I spoke with her parents in my office. We first discussed what it felt like to parent a child with an emotional dysregulation disorder. Anitra's parents said that it felt like they were unprepared, like they were "making it up" as they went. They had no idea what to say or do. They tried everything they could think of, and they did not know where to go for help. We acknowledged their profound feelings of helplessness and frustration. They loved their daughter and would do anything to help her.

Identifying and accepting the feelings of frustration and helplessness is a good first step toward taking a stance of validation. Once Anitra's parents identified their own feelings, they could take the next step of understanding what it meant for them to feel frustrated and helpless. When they understood the factors that contributed to their feeling helpless and frustrated, they could start to methodically address and remedy each one.

They felt unprepared. They learned to accept that their daughter suffered from a mood disorder that caused her to behave in ways that are disruptive. They accepted that if they could expect their daughter's struggle, they were less surprised and disappointed when her behavior got out of hand.

They felt ignorant. They educated themselves about mood disorders, depressive disorders, and anxiety. They asked questions of her providers, and joined a support group through the National Alliance for the Mentally Ill (NAMI) and networked with other parents sharing a similar experience. They learned how to share openly with their daughter about how they struggled with how to help her. Incidentally, when they shared with Anitra their own experience, they learned that she had the same frustrations and feelings.

They felt ineffective. They learned how to talk with her and how to help her heal. When they understood themselves better, they could help their daughter understand herself better.

When kids feel anxious, the well-meaning but uninformed adults around them often respond by saying things like, "There's nothing to worry about, just do your homework."

Parents have a tendency to ignore childhood worries and place their focus on completing tasks. As a result, they miss that their child is having a difficult time handling an experience, the details of which are not fully understood by the adult. A child may feel fearful or anxious or even have a disability (such as dyslexia) that causes them to get scared and nervous when they approach certain tasks.

Anxiety is a technical term to describe physical and emotional feelings of trepidation, worry, fright. Symptoms include thoughts of negative consequences, increased heart rate, sweaty palms, shortness of breath, a feeling of impending doom, and others. When parents minimize a child's anxiety, the child's self-esteem gets hurt. A child who is observant will look around and notice that other people don't seem nervous, and they may decide their anxiety is different or wrong. When they feel like something is wrong with them, they feel inadequate. When they feel inadequate, they tend to blame themselves for being wrong, not good enough, or different than others. When a child hates a part of themselves, their self-esteem plummets.

In an attempt to process their intense feelings of anxiety, kids might start to act very frustrated or irritable. They might become oppositional and start talking back. They may restrict their food. They may get stomachaches and headaches. They may sleep all the time to avoid activities that involve making connections with others. They may stay awake and become hyperactive and do risky things like running away or jumping off of the highest monkey bar. Most children can handle situational nerves with some help from their caregivers, but when those nerves become too overwhelming and they develop anxiety, then these children also need help from a mental health professional.

During my child psychiatry training, I evaluated a twelve-year-old boy living in a rural town in New Mexico. This boy, Robert, sat with his case-worker (from social services) across from me. He appeared to be neatly dressed, but did not smile, and offered little in terms of conversation other than a disdainful "yes," "no," or shrug of his shoulders. He glared often at me, and curled his lip. I struggled to make a connection with him. When I realized that I was entertaining strong feelings of dislike, I leaned back in my chair, took a deep breath, and made the conscious decision to set my reaction aside and focus on his symptoms and needs. When I did that, I was able to diagnose a major depressive disorder. He agreed, begrudgingly, to start an antidepressant (a selective serotonin reuptake inhibitor like sertraline) to curb his violent tendencies that stemmed from his anger at having endured physical abuse and at being in foster care. He left the office, and I felt like we had made a tenuous connection, if at all.

He returned four weeks later. This time, I immediately observed a big difference in his personality. He was affable, gentle, sweet, and funny. I could hardly believe he was the same boy I struggled to connect to a month ago! He was content, and not depressed anymore. He had been struggling with a severe serotonin deficiency, which caused him to not be able to handle stress and his own feelings. When that serotonin imbalance was corrected with medication, he was able to make the neural connections necessary to handle a great deal of stress. He could allow his true personality to shine so that we could get to the true matters at hand. He was truly a remarkably resilient and likeable boy.

When your child is struggling with depression, we must think of it as something for us to help manage. The diagnosis of major depression is not who the child is, nor does it define who the child can be. It's a brain disorder that people live with, and learn to cope with as it is part of them.

Situational nerves, or "the blues," have their momentary challenges too, like depression; however, one of the gifts of the blues is the ability to experience a range of feelings. Feeling sad and worried are indicators of the depth of sensitivity and empathy that is possible. It's beneficial in that it shows an individual their capability to empathize and connect with other people, and anticipate potential pitfalls to strategize how to avoid them. Situational nerves should pass when the situational cause is complete. Feelings of nerves in children can be triggered by disappointment, sensitivity, stress, or from the avoidance of feeling uncomfortable.

When a clinical depression hits, the child will experience profound and persistent sadness, irritability, lack of joy, inability to sleep or increased need for sleep, lack of appetite, low energy, difficulty concentrating, withdrawal from friends and usual activities, and feelings of guilt and hopelessness. The clinical symptoms present the challenges of depression, and need professional intervention to help a child resolve the clinical aspects of the disorder.

Depression presents an opportunity to address what it is our child is sensitive about, to understand how they are interpreting what's going on in their environment. This window into the depth of a child's feelings is a gift in that through therapy, the child can understand and appreciate a wide range and depth of feelings. When a child understands that they have this ability to get profoundly sad, they can start to notice earlier in situations that they are feeling sad, explore that sad feeling to determine what makes them sad and what they need, and then find ways to meet their needs before the overwhelming sadness consumes them. They can notice that they start to pull away and stop playing with their friends or family, or not want to play soccer, or have difficulty smiling or laughing. Once they learn how their depression starts, they can learn to realize, *I must be getting sad*, and start to get help to acknowledge their feelings. Adults need to help them with this by noticing that the child is showing symptoms of depression and by asking specific questions to draw out their feelings. The trick to helping your child heal from depression is to take your time and not get frustrated when you feel like you can't fix it for your kids.

"We don't understand what went wrong." Ethan's parents described a recent experience with their ten-year-old son who struggled with depression. "We took him to his best friend's birthday party this past weekend and everything went south."

Mom and Dad went on to explain that it was a children's party with a clown and a magician. Ethan looked like he was having much fun.

On the car ride home, Mom said, "The party was really fun, wasn't it?"

Ethan shrugged, and instantly became sullen and withdrawn.

His parents asked him, "What's wrong? Didn't you have fun at the party?"

They shared with me, "Every time we asked another question, he screamed, 'I hate you!' By the time we got home, he had completely shut down. He shoved his sister on the way in the house, ran into his room, slammed the door, and wouldn't talk to anybody. We just don't get it. At the party he was laughing, singing, and enjoying the magic show."

Not knowing what else to do, his parents left him to have a tantrum in his room. He cried himself to sleep and woke up feeling back to his usual depressive state: low energy, but no longer heightened.

Ethan's well-meaning parents could have benefited from the skills of validating and accepting Ethan's feelings, even when they didn't completely understand those feelings. After the party, instead of challenging Ethan's response—his non-verbal shrug, sullenness, and withdrawal—they could have asked another, more validating, question. This would have likely diffused his mood. When challenged, Ethan, like most children, became even more irritable and distant.

If Ethan's parents had made a reflective statement like, "You were laughing and it seemed to us that you were having fun. Did you feel the same way?" it may have engaged Ethan to recall the details of that moment and his experience, rather than put him on the defensive.

Reflective questions and statements help paint a picture of a specific moment or behavior for the child to recall. It is difficult for children to identify their feelings in any given moment, let alone remember them when asked about it. When they can't identify the feeling, they may struggle to remember the experience or vice versa. When in a depressive state, that recollection is hampered by their low mood, making it more difficult to identify happy feelings. In addition, if the child struggles with anxiety, it is the anxious state that is remembered, not the joyful feelings experienced during the party.

Why is it important to validate feelings for children who struggle with anxiety and depression? Feelings give us clues about our needs in any given moment. Feeling sad may indicate a need to cry, to remember a loss, to take a few minutes to be alone, or to acknowledge a disappointment. Feeling happy might mean that we enjoy something or someone, or appreciate a moment in time. It's virtually impossible to know what a feeling means to another person. The experience of happiness indicates something different for each person. We can't know what another might be feeling, and why it matters, unless we ask.

Knowing and understanding one's feelings can be a daunting task. For someone struggling with depression or anxiety, identifying a specific feeling can be even more confusing. At any given moment, all feelings coexist. Typically more powerful feelings like anger and irritability may overpower the more profound feelings of sadness and despair, making it a confusing mix of feelings too complex to accurately describe.

Depression and anxiety are not feelings. They are mood states determined by chemicals and neural connections in the brain. This concept is critical for parents to understand in order to help their children heal. This is important because it can help the child and parents realize that feelings will change. If parents can teach their child not to attach to whatever feeling is bothering them in any moment—knowing it will soon be replaced by another, like clouds in the sky—and if parents can teach their children to pay attention to how the wave of feeling feels in their body and mind, then children can learn about what gives them momentary happiness, sadness, or anger.

When parents and children learn what is driving a feeling, they can use that insight to develop coping skills from the experiences that generate happy feelings, or learn to resolve a situation that generates negative feelings. If Ethan can learn that interacting with his friends gives him happiness, then when he feels sad, he can use the coping skill of reaching out to his friends, or his parents can suggest that he meet up with a friend.

When parents can help their child tolerate their feeling of the current moment, children are free to move through their feelings rather than getting stuck in them. Parents have the opportunity to know that a feeling is not permanent. Children don't have the life experience of knowing that the feeling will pass. Adults do, and can model that tolerance of feelings for their child.

Since children do not have labels for each of their feelings, they may experience a multitude of feelings in any given moment, more so than adults. Adults have learned to understand a wide range of feelings and nuances of feelings, so it becomes easier to identify a particular feeling at a specific time. While one feeling may predominate in one moment, in the next moment another feeling may become stronger. This constant flux of feelings may be quite confusing for a child to decipher.

When a parent asks their child "how do you feel?" the child actually feels sad, happy, angry, scared, and joyful at the same time.

How does a ten-year-old child describe that experience? He shrugs his shoulders and replies, "I dunno."

The words "depression" and "anxiety" are often used to describe an experience, but they are a constellation of feelings, experiences, thoughts, neurology, psychological defenses, and physiological responses. When a tween feels anxious, she gets a surge of adrenaline, her heart beats faster, her breathing becomes shallow and quick, she may get tingling in her extremities; her eyes dilate, her muscles tense, and she may feel like fleeing. That's just the physiological response.

In her brain, her limbic system nerve cells fire and send signals of "I'm stressed, help!" Her psyche initiates her psychological defense mechanisms of irritability and guardedness, generating fear, avoidance and reaction. A reaction formation is making statements opposite of what she truly feels. When suffering from anxiety, she may feel insecure. She continually second guesses her choices, like repeatedly checking to see if she completed a task correctly. She may think that she is going crazy because her thoughts get stuck on one worry, and repeatedly mull over the worry. She will feel scared, sad, angry, irritable, elated, confused, and other feelings unique to each person.

When a tween is depressed, he struggles with not only sadness that does not go away, but also with a slowing down of body functions. He feels exhausted, lacks motivation, is unable to concentrate, feels pulled to stay in bed, avoids eye contact, speaks softly, moves slowly, thinks slower than usual, loses his appetite, and wants to disengage with the world because he simply cannot imagine that his experience can get better.

I explained to Ethan's parents that even though he is diagnosed with depression, he will still have momentary feelings of happiness and enjoyment. It means that overall his mood state is depressed. While he experiences situations that temporarily distract him from his depression, like at a fun birthday party with friends, he can look like he's happy and having a good time. As soon as that situation ends, he goes back to his typical mood state, which is depressed. This can be confusing for parents who may expect an enjoyable experience to last longer than the event.

Children feel pressure to act and feel whatever they think the adults around them expect them to. All children feel this parental pressure but, unlike healthy children, depressed children cannot raise their low state on their own. For that reason, they feel even more irritable and frustrated because they can't change how they feel. All children desire to please their parents. They want to maintain the connection with their parents so any time they feel they are failing to please their parents or meet their expectations, it makes them feel especially bad about themselves. At times like this, it is important for parents to validate the child's actual experience and practice tolerating uncomfortable feelings with their child. This practice allows for the child to experience learning how to tolerate their feelings, and it prevents them from feeling guilty for not meeting a parental expectation. A child who is struggling with a depression or anxiety disorder may not experience the same sadness or excitement that their parent is feeling.

Acknowledging feelings benefits both parents and children, especially those struggling with anxiety and depression. Depression and anxiety are biological illnesses. There are many messages out there saying, "Just ignore your feelings and do something you like, then your mood will change." That's helpful for someone who's having momentary blues or situational nerves or dealing with an upsetting situation, but we can't expect our depressed child to just go outside, throw the ball around, and feel better. Depression is caused by a shortage of chemicals in the brain that influences mood. Serotonin levels are relatively lower in children struggling with depression. It's more difficult for neurons to make connections in the brain that induces them to feel better. Neurons communicate with each other through neurotransmitters like serotonin. When there's not enough transmitters transferred between neurons there's not enough to send a message. In a depressed state, because there's not as much serotonin available, the pathways for feeling better can't make enough of a connection and the child remains in the depressed state.

When we understand and validate what a child is experiencing, we help a child reduce their frustration about not meeting the expectations of their parents to feel something different. Once validated, children are more accepting of themselves, and can allow for their internal strengths and cognitive abilities to do their magic. They can allow the sadness to dissipate and the child becomes less irritable. From that place of calmness, they can think more clearly about what they want to do. When kids are in a heightened state of emotion like sadness, fear, anger, anxiety, or even elation, they can get easily overwhelmed, and make unhealthy decisions. They are more prone to thoughts of harming themselves or other people. They are more likely to have suicidal thoughts and plans. Many children cut or burn themselves when they're feeling overwhelmed by sadness and despair, and desperately want to feel some relief. They get to a point of wanting so badly to feel better that they believe they must act on that feeling.

By accepting your child's feelings and understanding that they are changeable, you help her understand and learn that she can accept her feelings. She doesn't have to change them; therefore, she doesn't have to hurt herself. Together you can practice accepting the feeling, tolerating it, and then allowing that uncomfortable moment to pass.

Had Ethan's parents understood how to validate his feelings, I believe his post–birthday party upset would not have escalated into him screaming, crying, and pushing his sister. The first opportunity for his parents to validate his feelings came when they noticed him becoming sullen and withdrawn.

Had they said something like "seems like the birthday party was fun," without adding any assumptions about his feelings, but just giving him a hug or sitting next to him, they could have prevented the escalation of his irritability. In addition, those moves would lessen the chance of Ethan getting frustrated at himself for not being able to maintain a better mood. A child can feel alone when he realizes that everyone around him seems to be having more fun and able to sustain their enjoyment of the activity.

CHAPTER 2

Anxiety and Depression in Tweens

Everyone experiences situational nerves and the blues. Nervousness is useful in that it motivates us to change and move forward. It motivates us to make goals and to take the steps needed to achieve those goals. Nerves can also show us where we feel hesitant to embark on something new, like meeting a new person. We can use nervousness as our internal orange warning flag that sends us the message, *Hey, take it a little slower here*. It gives us clues about how we feel inside and what we need to feel safe and secure in any given situation. When we get to know our nervousness and welcome it as we would a friend, it can teach us about ourselves. If we try to ignore our nerves or stuff it down, it can come back to us multifold. Nerves are there to help us, essentially saying, *I'm here to help you, but if you try to get rid of me I'm going to fight to stay here.*

Lucy's parents called on a Friday morning looking for an appointment that day. Thankfully, we had a space in the afternoon. When Lucy, a nine-year-old girl, and her mother walked into my office, I could immediately feel the tension. Lucy told me that for two weeks she had felt increasingly more stressed and she thought "something bad" was going to happen to her.

She leaned forward, looked directly into my eyes and stated, "I think I need to go to the hospital, I just can't stand it anymore."

She explained that her parents fought all the time.

She went on, "They yell and scream all the time and they hate each other."

She continued to tearfully say, "I am afraid they are going to get divorced."

After a few moments, her father entered the room. Lucy shoved him away from her. At that point, I asked the parents to stay in the room, and asked Lucy to go to the playroom. She quietly agreed.

As I listened, Lucy's parents explained their marital conflict. They argued even as they affirmed their commitment to the marriage. I couldn't help but wonder why they were still together. They seemed passionate about their disagreements, but lacked compassion for each other's point of view. I felt a sense of urgency, and fear inside of me. I was not sure if this couple's tension would come to blows. As I sat and listened, tolerating the anxiety building inside of me, I realized that these parents were passionate people and expressed themselves loudly and pointedly. Despite their obvious verbal escalation, their behavior was consistently appropriate and non-threatening. The more they argued, the more their bodies relaxed. I could relate to the fear and anxiety Lucy must have been feeling whenever her parents began to verbally disagree with each other…I was feeling it firsthand!

Though her parents argued as a way to dissipate their tension and their conflicts, for Lucy, their heated energy overwhelmed and overpowered her young psyche's ability to manage. The uncertainty of her parent's situation scared her. In this case, Lucy's parents sought my assistance to help her not feel anxious about their situation. However, the solution was not to change Lucy's ability to tolerate stress. She was having a normal and reasonable response to her parents' arguing style. The solution was for her parents to understand that Lucy, like most children, could not tolerate the level of intensity of adult conflicts. I recommended that they take their conflicts out of earshot of their daughter.

Lucy's parents brought her in believing she had anxiety and

depression, but she was suffering from situational nerves. Many parents try to look outside themselves and their own issues for help reaching their distant child. When some parents see that their efforts are not working, they will enlist the help of other family and friends. Parents may think that the child is tired of hanging out with them so they arrange time with grandparents or other relatives. When that doesn't work, they try to arrange playdates. Exasperated, some parents resort to saying, "Snap out of it!" or "You're just having a pity party."

Others will attempt to add exercise or change the diet to improve their child's mood. Some of these changes are helpful, but ultimately children diagnosed with depression or anxiety will remain unable to access the motivation or desire to fully engage in their lives. If these efforts don't work, many parents will then take their children to non–mental health providers like a dietitian, chiropractor, or acupuncturist. These too are good ideas; however, they rarely work on their own. This is because many parents don't understand the seriousness of the depressive process or anxiety. All these interventions fail to get at the root of the problem; they treat only the symptoms of the illness. Another reason these interventions may not work is that many of these interventions are geared toward adults. A child's brain is still developing, so each healing intervention needs to be considered in the context of a child's psychological, physical, and cognitive development. Lucy's parents would not have known had they not brought her in.

Following are the most common statements I hear from parents of children struggling with anxiety and depression:

"I feel like my child is slipping away from me."

"I feel helpless about how to support my child."

"I can't reach my child"

"I'm afraid to discipline my depressed/anxious child."

"I don't know what to say or do in challenging situations."

Carmen was in eighth grade. She loved art, sports, and school. When her mother brought her into my office, she said, "I don't understand, she gets straight As in school and is very good at sports and is an excellent artist. But lately she has not been doing any of the things she loves. I tried to get her to go to lacrosse practice and she won't go. She loves volleyball, and I can't get her to go to that either."

She continued, "I've tried to get her to hang out with her friends or go shopping with me, which used to bring her so much joy. She won't do any art either, and she was passionate about her artwork."

Carmen's mother showed me some of her artwork. It was truly amazing for a twelve-year-old. It was at the level of a professional artist.

"She's not interested in it and doesn't think it's any good," her mother continued. "When I compliment her about how great she is, she just goes into her room and shuts the door."

Mom shared that school mornings are especially rough. She tries to get Carmen out of bed, but she doesn't want to go to school. The principal, her teachers, and her friends love her, but she has convinced herself that nobody likes her.

In an effort to reach out to her daughter, Carmen's mom tried things that many parents do in an attempt to reach their depressed or anxious child. Even though she was a busy professional, she agreed to spend more time at home with her daughter. She also tried taking her daughter to work with her. She offered to go to all of her sporting events and practices. She offered to arrange carpools. She cut back on her office hours, so that she could be more available to her child. She offered to do whatever activities her daughter chose on the weekends. Still, Carmen did not want to do anything.

The good news is that underneath their anxiety or depression, your child is still the same person. Nothing has been lost. They still have all the wonderful qualities they always had. However, depression is a brain disorder, and puts a heavy filter, or cloud, over their personality and ability to interact with others. All of their unique qualities remain untouched, though hidden. Who they are, their personality, is still there, though the depressive cloud makes it hard to get through. When you lift the cloud, who they are can burst through. What it takes to lift the cloud is to treat the depressive or anxiety disorder at its core in the brain. It's not enough to treat symptoms with diet or exercise. The core of anxiety and depression is biological and psychological so we need to work at those levels if a child is to heal. I encourage parents to have confidence in their parenting and their bond throughout the treatment process. The work they have done to build their attachment to their child is still active. It feels frustrating and discouraging, but I tell parents, "Trust that the connection is still there and waiting for you to enjoy again."

Lucy's parents enjoyed a connection with their daughter simply by changing their behavior while Carmen's mother had to work a stricter protocol to get that connection.

Children who struggle with depression and anxiety are highly sensitive to how their parents deliver guidance and discipline. A child who does not struggle with anxiety or depression, on the other hand, can tolerate more common discipline techniques including a firm tone of voice or their parents giving them "the look." These children understand that they did something that they should not have done. They understand that the parent is displeased with their behavior and, most importantly, they do not take it personally. A child who is anxious or depressed experiences these kinds of discipline differently. Depressed and anxious children have a heightened sensitivity to perceived personal rejection or any kind of negativity. When parents go about enforcing boundaries or the rules in the home, the depressed child often views this type of parenting as hurtful. They understand on an intellectual level that their parent is setting reasonable expectations. They understand, but they cannot tolerate it emotionally. Because of their heightened sensitivity, they will react to discipline they perceive as harsh with crying, irritability, or feelings of numbness. In short, they emotionally crumble.

Once a child starts to crumble, many parents start to feel guilty, like they have done something wrong to their child. Because they don't know what to do or how to discipline their depressed or anxious child, they apologize: "I'm so sorry. I didn't mean it." At that point, the effectiveness of the discipline has been lost. Over time, parents feel increasingly guilty and uncertain. They feel they can no longer enforce boundaries and limits. This in turn makes the child feel unsafe. Children need boundaries. Though they may not say it, children need their parents to guide them and enforce the rules. Yet, it is challenging for parents to provide that safe and supportive space when these children are sensitive to the customary ways of parenting and disciplining.

When parents devise a plan for discipline, they need to understand that the anxious or depressed child feels alone and insecure, and may struggle with their level of self-esteem. Also, because of their disorder, they can quickly become debilitated and not be able to function. They may not be able to physically motivate themselves to complete the task, to follow a rule, or to be fully present in a conversation.

HOW TO DISCIPLINE

Always take care of yourself before approaching your child with corrective information. Unless you take care of yourself, it is challenging to feel centered enough to take care of your child. The first thing parents need to do is to take a few deep breaths. The more deep breaths you take, the easier it is to feel calm.

Say to yourself, "I love my child more than anything in the world. I can do this. I can calm myself down. I can put aside my frustration and irritability."

Seat yourself physically on the same side of the child, not in front of your child. Sitting next to a child while facing the same direction is a physical tangible experience of "being on the same side." When you start on the same side, it is a lot easier to create the emotional and cognitive experience of working together toward a goal. The goal is to understand, help, and assist them, not to lecture them. They interpret telling them to do something as confrontational. When they feel confronted, they can shut down in a nanosecond.

Once your child has calmed, then you may begin to talk about the situation or displeasing behaviors. You might start by saying something like, "We need to discuss what happened this morning. Is now an okay time for us to have that discussion?"

If your child says, "No, I don't want to talk about it," and seems tearful, irritable, or forlorn, accept it and say, "Okay, but we need to discuss it, so let's try for later today."

If your child looks up and makes eye contact with you, and does not seem to be emotionally upset, you may say, "We really do need to talk, because it's something that needs to be addressed. I would like us to talk now."

When we can discipline using the principles of validation, the conversation often progresses toward understanding each person's experience. This does not mean that parents walk on eggshells around their child, and it does not mean that children need to be tentative and unsure of themselves. It means that parents and children approach each other with confidence and vulnerability, expecting mutual respect and empathy at each interaction. Sitting side by side allows for parents and children to hold hands, cuddle, or give side hugs. For children struggling with depression and anxiety, this closeness and accessibility to their parent's support and love is crucial to help the child feel secure and safe.

When Anitra behaved in a defiant manner, her parents learned to sit with her and ask, "What happened?"

She replied, "I dunno."

Her parents continued maintaining a soft, gentle tone of voice, "Anitra, you are our sweet, good girl. There must be something going on that is hard to handle. Let's talk about it."

With patience and gentle nudging to express her feelings and experience, Anitra's parents came to understand that earlier that day Anitra had a negative encounter with one of her friends. She felt rejected and sad. When Anitra was able to share her feelings, express her disappointment, and feel her parents' empathy, she was also able to apologize for her defiant behavior.

This approach to discipline works because children inherently want to please their parents, and their misbehavior is generally a product of confusion and inability to handle their feelings, rather than a deliberate behavior. Anitra's parents did not have to address the act of bad behavior, as it was resolved during the process of understanding and supporting the experiences that led up to the behavior.

When a child's depression or anxiety gets out of control, they feel emotionally overwhelmed and do not know how to relieve the intense pain that is caused by depression and anxiety. The pain is felt in their body as well as in their psyche. In these situations, they can start thinking and talking about self-harm. Hearing that your child is considering harming themselves is one of the most painful things a parent can experience. This is when parents share with me that they feel the most helpless.

One of the most common questions I hear from parents about their child who is cutting themselves or making statements that they want to die is "are they serious or are they just looking for attention?" The answer is both. Their child is serious about feeling lost, empty, and distressed to the point of not knowing how else to find relief except for hurting themselves. They are seeking attention; they need attention and assistance to relieve their profound emotional pain.

I met a thirteen-year-old girl named Janey at the Children's Psychiatric Hospital shortly after she had been taken to the seclusion room. I was the doctor on call, so I was asked to see her. She had just taken her shaving razor and cut high up on her thighs. This cutting behavior was not new to her. She was admitted to the psychiatric hospital after attempting to kill herself by cutting her wrists, and she had made some significant cuts. The cuts she made to her thighs on this day, two days after admission, were fairly superficial, but caused a lot of bleeding and distress for her nurse and staff. As I spoke with her, she said that she had gotten upset with a peer and immediately cut on herself with the most readily available object. We talked through her distress and she felt settled after a few moments and returned to be with her peers. I advised the staff to help Janey through her moments of distress by offering her outlets for her pain, as follows: a walk around the playground, time in the seclusion room to vent (scream, kick, or cry), or a listening ear. Janey had not learned any strategies for managing her uncomfortable feelings, and needed almost moment-to-moment guidance.

As adults, we often fall into the belief that others, including children, should be able to handle their feelings, and then do not offer that moment-to-moment guidance and support that they actually need. This automatic response by adults is not because we don't care, but due to common beliefs and expectations that children be more independent than they are. Janey, the next day, became distressed during a game of Blokus, and tried to swallow a plastic game piece, which lodged in the back of her mouth. The staff immediately jumped on her to attempt to stop her from swallowing it and, in the process, the piece got lodged even deeper. An emergency response team was called, and they used a laryngoscope to remove the game piece from her throat. She had no injuries, but she was then placed in the Behavioral Intensive Care Unit with two to three staff watching her twenty-four hours a day. The intention of having her in the Behavioral Intensive Care Unit was to decrease stimulation and opportunities to seek attention from peers and others.

Little is more distressing to a parent than realizing that their child is harming themselves and having serious thoughts and wishes to die. Their natural inclination is to try to take control of the situation and prevent further physical harm. Unfortunately, well-intentioned parents often misunderstand why children harm themselves. Children harm themselves because they do not know how else to handle their immense pain and emptiness. Cutting, self-harm, and suicidal ideations are all coping mechanisms. These are unhealthy, but they offer some relief, if only for a moment. Not only does trying to physically control the situation miss the underlying reason for self-harm, it is ineffective and can lead to further harm.

Children (and adults) need a way to cope with distress. If a reliable (albeit unhealthy) coping mechanism is taken away without giving another (healthy) coping mechanism, the child will become desperate to use existing unhealthy coping mechanisms. While Janey was in the seclusion area with two to three staff watching her at all times, she managed to use her fingernails to scratch under the elastic on her pants. She made such a deep scratch that she developed an infection which entered her abdomen. Only when she started to spike fevers were the scratches and infection discovered. At that point, she needed to be transferred to the intensive care unit (ICU) at the main hospital for IV antibiotics. She was there for over five days, and nearly died.

Janey's case is an extreme situation, but illustrates how powerful the feeling of desperation can be for children to relieve their emotional pain in the only way they know how. Janey was missing the opportunity to receive reflective questions from a caregiver to help her understand the source of her frustration; tolerate her feelings of rejection, helplessness, and loneliness; and help her develop a new coping mechanism like expressing her feelings and talking to peers who support her.

While many children will use cutting on their bodies as a coping mechanism to relieve deep emotional hurts, few children actually want to die while cutting. The children who cut may also have suicidal ideations from time to time, but the purpose of their habitual cutting is due to seeking relief, not a result of wanting to die. Children do not make superficial cuts on a regular basis with the intention of working toward a fatal cut. They make cuts to relieve pain, and may accidentally cut too much or too deep, which puts them at risk of unintentionally attempting suicide.

In fact, the suicidal ideation that most children struggle with is a desire "to not be here anymore," not a desire to actively kill themselves.

The desire is a passive wish.

Children often tell me, "I wouldn't mind if something happened and I just left or wasn't here anymore."

Children often do not use the word "die" until they are very serious, and when they say that they want to die, their risk of attempting to kill themselves is high. If intervention is utilized before they start to talk about wanting to die, and children find relief through positive coping mechanism which can be taught, then the suicidal ideation typically goes away. However, if no intervention is offered, then the wish to not be here anymore can become a more active thought of, "I am going to do something to make myself go away." Children like Janey are crying out for help.

Thankfully, there is a way out of this emotional roller coaster. How parents present limits, discipline, and boundaries to their depressed or anxious child is important. A child with depression and anxiety requires more explanation, a sort of prelude to discipline.

Eleven-year-old William forgot to take the trash out.

When his father got home from work and found the trash bins full, he said, "You didn't take the trash out. You're grounded, you can't go to your friend's party this weekend."

A depressed and anxious child cannot emotionally tolerate this kind of negative language (words such as "can't" and "didn't") and the disappointed tone. When a child struggles with depression or anxiety, parents need to be extra gentle and begin the conversation by calmly saying something like, "Let's talk about what happened. Do you remember that I had asked you about taking out the trash?" Disciplining kids with depression and anxiety takes more time, explanation, and sharing of feelings. The faster we accept that truth and meet their needs, the more peaceful everyone will feel.

CHAPTER 3

My Child's Brain

ADHD, or attention deficit hyperactivity disorder, is a neurodevelopmental disorder that affects 11 percent of children ages four to seventeen in America, about 6.4 million children (according to the Centers for Disease Control). It is the most widely diagnosed psychiatric illness in children and adolescents. ADHD is often diagnosed in childhood and may persist into adulthood.

Children with ADHD are usually hyperactive, inattentive, impulsive, and easily distracted; they interrupt others, have difficulty focusing on the task at hand, and can't concentrate. There are three subtypes: predominantly inattentive, predominantly hyperactive, and a combined type. Kids who struggle with ADHD of the predominantly inattentive type are often overlooked because they are not disruptive in the classroom or at home. Trying to manage ADHD is difficult for a child. Many parents get frustrated with children who display symptoms of ADHD; these children often also struggle with depressive and anxiety disorders. Depression can run as high as 60 percent in children with ADHD. Anxiety disorders run around 30 percent in children diagnosed with ADHD. There may be genetic factors also linked to ADHD with depression and anxiety.

Jonah struggles with significant ADHD and serious episodes of depression. His strategies for dealing with his ADHD required a lot of time and energy, particularly when it came to completing his school assignments. As a result of his inability to stay focused, his grades had dropped for the previous two years despite being highly intelligent. The school considered holding him back to repeat seventh grade, but decided to let him advance to the next grade if he agreed to make up his missing work over the summer. He agreed, as he very much wanted to move ahead with his class. He struggled. In order to get his work done, Jonah had no social life during his summer break. He didn't see his friends, he felt lonely, and his mood dropped as the summer progressed.

When I spoke to his parents about strategies to deal with his ADHD, Jonah was completely on board, but his mother's only response was, "My husband and I spend too much time telling him to do his work, reminding him when his homework is due, and nagging him to put it in his backpack and take it to school. When does that stop?"

Jonah's parents were not in tune to his struggles. His mother was fixated on when she could stop telling him what to do. While she talked to me about her needs, I watched Jonah lean back, slump in his chair, and close his eyes. He checked out of the conversation. Mom spoke about how she could maintain her goals and agenda with no indication of any desire to compromise for his goals and agenda. I explained to Mom that, though I understood her frustration, she would need to continue to remind her son about what was needed and how to organize his tasks, because the executive functioning skills in kids with ADHD are slower to develop. Executive functioning skills include higher cognitive processing—like organizing time, data, and thoughts—and the ability to plan and anticipate what might be needed to complete any course of action. Even though kids with ADHD are typically very intelligent, they develop these skills later than their peers. A ten-step process to organize a plan for kids without ADHD becomes a thirty-step process for a child who struggles with ADHD.

I explained to Jonah's mom that the first step in healing for her son would be for her and her husband to help lighten the load around Jonah's focus and concentration issues. Until he is able to focus better, she and her husband would need to continue to play that role for him. I encouraged her to move from focusing on their impatience and resentment about performing these functions to accepting that this is part of parenting a child with ADHD. She could help in his development and his healing of his ADHD if she could willingly assume the role of planner and organizer until her son's brain could catch up. I went on to explain that this strategy of becoming more supportive could also help prevent the depressive episodes that are triggered by his frustration and disappointment. Jonah's mom cares very much about her son and was invested in solving his problems.

Mom was focusing on Jonah's grades and his curtailed social life (results). The part she was missing was that he was exerting a tremendous amount of effort trying to get his work done (what's going on inside). She saw him staying up late and not seeing friends, but she could not see (or appreciate) the amount of energy it took him to complete his homework. In working with Jonah's mother, I encouraged her to accept the role of becoming his executive functioning support and at the same time I encouraged her to understand that his brain would develop those executive planning skills; for now, she needed to do his planning for him.

Understanding how a child's brain develops can help us understand how to help our child when they struggle with emotional or behavioral challenges. The brain undergoes rapid growth during pregnancy and increases through the first six years of life. After that rapid growth period, the brain still forms new neurons (brain cells), but after about age six, our brain is involved in the process of shaping neural pathways rather than growing new cells. It is this shaping process that is important to learn about, because when parents understand how the brain and its pathways are formed, they can promote emotional healing and provide needed structure.

Ninety percent of a person's brain volume is formed by the time they are six years old. This means that in the brains of children younger than six, the brain grows in response to genetic predisposition, and to stimuli from the child's environment. The brains of children older than six are being pruned and shaped according to their experiences; every interaction and situation affects the way the brain makes neural pathways. For instance, when a child touches a hot object, the nerves in the hand send a signal to the brain, the brain makes note that the object is hot, and then sends a signal to remove the hand to prevent a burn. This is an example of how a neural pathway is created. The next time the child touches a hot object, the pathway is set and they will remove their hand quicker.

The brain matures by developing connections between major functional areas. All these connections and pathways dictate how your child thinks, feels, and behaves. Initially, the brain cells make connections all over the brain similar to a spider web. It starts out small and over time the brain sends out another arm of the web and touches another cell. It's like two hands connecting. Specific cells will maintain certain connections, or remove connections based on a child's experiences. For example, children who are exposed to different languages early in childhood develop the ability to learn those languages throughout their lifetime more so than a child who is exposed to a single language in the home. This is due to developing a pattern of connections between nerve cells in the language areas of the brain, so that when a new language is recognized, the brain has pathways already set up to receive that language and begin to learn it.

When a child's brain is presented with an experience (or set of stimuli), the brain reacts to that set of stimuli and is challenged to make neural connections. Those connections allow the brain to take in the stimuli and process it, so that the brain can do something with the experience, like remember it, analyze it, and initiate a course of action. When a child's brain is continually exposed to a similar set of stimuli, it develops a set of pathways that becomes a more permanent part of the brain that is activated each time a similar experience occurs. In the case of the child exposed to many languages, for the rest of his life when he is confronted by a new set of verbal patterns, his brain will automatically activate that part of his brain which knows how to handle and learn an unknown language.

Mental health professionals help shape the brain and form

healthy connections. This is what they are up to during each moment of their work with your child. While you may notice that your child makes better choices, manages their emotions better, and focuses better in school, the changes health professionals focus on are the changes that are made at the cell level in your child's brain. These changes that happen as a result of therapy last throughout the rest of a child's life. These cellular changes do not need to occur only during a one-hour-per-week session with a therapist, however. Parents, teachers, caregivers, and anyone interacting with children can learn to set the stage for healing and provide experiences to encourage healthy brain shaping and healing. In short, anyone can learn how to grow a healthier brain.

Imagine a bonsai tree growing wild and untouched. One day a gardener comes along and prunes certain areas to create a distinct shape. That's similar to what shaping does to the brain. When a child enters kindergarten or preschool, they learn how to interact with other kids and follow the rules of the classroom. In the healthy brain, the child learns and acts appropriately according to what is expected of him. For instance, he learns that teachers expect children to line up after recess to return to the classroom. The brain takes in the information of the teacher saying, "Time to line up," and connects that auditory cue to the part of the brain that decodes the words, understands the action required, then sends signals to the motor areas of the brain which coordinates the behavior of lining up with his peers. The healthy brain says, *The teacher said "line up," what does that mean to me? Oh, I know how to do that*, and then chooses the appropriate behavior.

In a healthy child, you may notice that initially, when he first hears the command to line up, he may wander around the playground for a few moments, but over time he will make his way over to the line. After a few days, a child with healthy brain connections will immediately go over and get in line. His brain has experienced shaping. In the best case scenario, a child gets enough positive pruning experiences early in life to be able to handle most demands in life. Even if that is not the case, a child's brain can be reshaped. The encouraging news is that therapists and parents alike have the power to shape a child's brain into a healthy configuration.

Children diagnosed with anxiety or depression may start with a brain that develops normally, but then something happens, either their genetics or an event triggers a halt or slowing of typical development. Children may get worried, then get overwhelmed and not know how to handle the situation. *My mom is sick and that makes me very sad, angry, and confused and I don't know how to deal with that.* The brain goes haywire trying to make connections until it finds one that fits or works, or it is simply unable to make enough of a connection due to low levels of neurotransmitters (i.e. serotonin, dopamine, or norepinephrine) to transmit a signal from one cell to another. When the brain cannot make adequate connections, then depression and anxiety symptoms start to appear.

Depression and anxiety often go hand in hand, creating symptoms that are confusing, contradictory, and seemingly out of control. The brain, through trial and error, attempts to figure out a pathway to initiate a behavior or response; *if I just ignore it then maybe I will feel better* is one possible outcome. Another is to "act out" by becoming oppositional and defiant. If those strategies don't work, children may feel even more insecure and uncertain. The younger the child, the more body-centered their reactions will be, including throwing tantrums, digging in their heels, refusing to budge, hitting walls or others, banging their head, and slamming doors. An older child is more likely to become argumentative, withdrawn, or both. As the child's cognition matures and the brain is able to make more connections and healthy pathways, they will be able to see more options, become less reactive, and be able to manage and express their needs.

It's not just what happens in the therapist's office that shapes your child's brain and promotes healing. Each and every interaction parents have works to shape a child's developing brain. Coupled with medication to address the chemical imbalances that lead to ineffective connections, the experiences parents give their child can have a lasting impact. When we understand this, we empower ourselves to be a part of the healing team, a true Healer Parent.

When people come to see me, it's usually because their pediatrician, primary care physician, therapist, teacher, or family member referred them for a medication evaluation. When kids are referred under that label, their parents experience a variety of reactions. Sometimes parents feel validated by the label, but that's less common. I find more often parents are quite nervous about their child needing a medication evaluation because it conjures up fears and stigma about mental illness. When a parent comes for our first appointment, they usually start talking about how they don't want their child on Ritalin or Prozac. They are focused on the negative media attention and catchphrases like "children are overmedicated." They often quote the media hype, including *Prozac Nation*, or insist that Ritalin is being "handed out like candy." Parents come in with a whole set of biases about what it means for their child to be on medications. When they come in with a strong bias and preconceived ideas, they can often lose sight of the purpose of the evaluation process.

I am a medical doctor which makes me different than a psychologist, social worker, and therapist. I am one puzzle piece of a comprehensive team that is here to support your child. I am trained to administer therapy, and sometimes do. I am a medical doctor who is schooled in diagnosing disorders and developing a comprehensive treatment plan, which includes prescribing medication, if necessary, for children, tweens, and teens with mental and behavioral issues. I work in conjunction with your tween's therapist, and school counselor.

Instead of using the terminology "medication evaluation," I would call it an assessment of mental health needs. Parents would be more likely to come in with an open mind. I imagine they would be more willing to have their child see a psychiatrist for a general evaluation of their mental health needs and the family's mental health needs. Through the assessment process, we might determine that medication would be helpful. When that determination is made, what we are looking at is seeing if medication, in conjunction with other therapies, will help bring about well-being and improve mental health.

Medication is used for the purpose of managing the biological aspects of a mental illness such as depression, anxiety, ADHD, mood disorders, or psychotic disorders. It's not the end-all, but it can be helpful as a support to healing.

I completed an evaluation of a twelve-year-old girl who came in with her mother on the bequest of herself. She had told her pediatrician that she was having panic attacks and feeling sad, anxious, and depressed. Initially, the mother had asked the pediatrician for help. The pediatrician referred them to me. When I evaluated the mother and daughter, mom had several questions about medications and wasn't sure what the child needed in terms of medication and/or therapy. The child, on the other hand, had done quite a bit of research about anxiety and depression. She had read about therapy and medication and came in open to starting medication if it was going to help her.

This young girl was open with me about all her symptoms and felt encouraged and hopeful about getting treatment. After I did an assessment, I determined that she had a generalized anxiety disorder and clinical depression. I suggested that they consider beginning a medication like Prozac, Zoloft, or other selective serotonin reuptake inhibitor (SSRI).

The mother was worried and said, "I heard that antidepressants can cause children to become suicidal."

I addressed her concern by letting her know that the risk of becoming suicidal was not a common risk. The actual risk was that one in ten thousand young people under the age of twenty-six have an increased risk of having more suicidal thoughts. This risk is greatest in the first month of treatment or in the first month after increasing the dose of medication. This is rare and if it does happen, the feelings last about a day or so and I don't expect it to lead to suicidal activity unless the diagnosis is incorrect. It can lead to more thoughts about dying and it is scary when children have these thoughts, because they can get preoccupied about suicide during that time. They don't necessarily have plans or intentions to carry out suicidal thoughts. When children have those thoughts, I ask the parents to reassure their child, provide increased supervision, and make sure they call me or the therapist. If parents let us know what's going on, we can evaluate the scenario and offer them reassurance.

Parents can also provide supervision, such as allowing their child to sleep in their room, or spending the day together. The thoughts are not controllable, and will not go away with interventions or with coping methods. Parents and children must wait until the thoughts subside. The suicidal thoughts usually stop after about twenty-four hours. If they don't, we may decrease the dosage or change to another antidepressant. If a child gets those suicidal thoughts with one antidepressant, it's not necessarily true they will get suicidal thoughts with another antidepressant.

Sometimes a child will become afraid of this too, but usually the child has already read about it and feels pretty confident they will tell their parents or their therapist that they are having those thoughts. They are often willing to take on the risk in order to feel better because they recognize how much they suffer with depression or anxiety on a daily basis.

Types of questions parents often have are regarding other short-term side effects. Side effects typically include headaches and stomach upset. These go away after a few days. They also have questions about long-term side effects and I'm happy to report that there are zero reported long-term side effects with the SSRI antidepressants. There are a couple of medications that do have long term side effects including weight gain and increased triglycerides, but these are more specialized medications and not used first for the treatment of anxiety and depression. The common SSRIs, including Prozac, Celexa, Zoloft, Lexapro, and Paxil, have no long-term side effects.

For most parents, once they are educated about the specific expectations regarding side effects, they are keener on starting an antidepressant. I make a strong point of talking to parents about the expected course of treatment with the SSRI antidepressants that are typically prescribed for anxiety and depression. It's almost universal how people react to the medications.

During the first couple weeks of taking a medication like Prozac or Zoloft, the medication gives a boost of serotonin to the brain. For those first couple of weeks people feel like the cloud has lifted and think they might have found the cure for their depression. It would be great if it were this easy, but the way the brain works is that it accommodates to a new condition. The cells always want to go back to what is normal for them, also known as homeostasis. What's happening those first two weeks is not normal, so the cells accommodate by making even more receptors to take all the serotonin out of the space between two nerve cells.

The brain says, "I know there's too much serotonin in here. I'd better get all that out of here and get back to normal."

Two weeks after this high, nearly every patient I have, comes into my office and says, "It's not working anymore. We need to try something else."

They get discouraged. I have to remind them about how the medication works and encourage them that unless they are having serious or intolerable side effects, they need to be extraordinarily patient. The brain will adjust to a new normal if you continue to take the medication.

If you continue to take the medication, the brain continues to get a flood of serotonin and after a period of time, about thirty to sixty days, the brain gets used to this and says, essentially, "Wait a minute, am I supposed to be having this amount of serotonin?" and it readjusts to be able to use all the serotonin that's there. It starts to change the ratio of receptors and it starts to make more serotonin itself. In about four to six weeks patients start to feel better again. The change is not quite as dramatic as during the first two weeks; it's more subtle, but it's more long-lasting.

Patients will say to me, "I think it's working again. I'm not worrying so much."

If patients can get through the first four to six weeks, often the effect is close to what we want it to be.

Sometimes parents will ask me, "If the medication is not going to start working for six to eight weeks, why do we need to see you before that time?"

I explain, "I need to see your child at two to four weeks. I know, through experience, that I need to continue to facilitate the successful experience with the medication. I need to encourage your child to continue to take the medication."

I remind parents and children about the pattern of the peak and the slump that precedes the resolution. I also check for side effects. It's essential for a child's success that families see their psychiatrist frequently during the first couple of months until the depressive or anxiety disorder has resolved.

While trying to find the right medication and dose to treat my young patient, parents' impatience can get overwhelming, and fall into a Fix-It Parent pattern. The Fix-It Parent makes decisions on their own without consulting their psychiatrist or expressing their concerns. Some Fix-It Parents start their child's medication at a level other than the suggested dosage. I ask patients to start the first five to seven days of medication at a dosage lower than the therapeutic dose. This is important to help the body get used to the medication and minimize side effects. Sometimes, the Fix-It Parent skips this step and goes straight to the therapeutic dose. When this happens, their child often suffers unnecessary side effects such as a headache or a stomachache, because the higher dosage is too abrupt for the body to handle. We have problems after this happens, as a child is often resistant to starting medication again. It becomes nearly impossible to regain a child's trust and cooperation after they experience unpleasant side effects and difficult to get them to start the medication again or try another medication.

Another thing the Fix-It Parent does is change doses on their own. They might start with the half dose and go to the full dose at the two-week point. They might increase the dosage after their child has entered into the natural and expected slump of moods. These parents want to just skip the unpleasantness and boost their child's mood immediately. Unfortunately, the brain doesn't work this way and often has to accommodate even more, which increases the risk of side effects. Eventually, the Fix-It Parent makes the unilateral decision that the medication doesn't work and the medication, not to mention their child's recovery, never gets a fair trial. If we play out this scenario with too many medications, then we run out of the safest options for treating the child. Fix-It Parents sabotage their child's success by stopping the medication prematurely.

Sometimes a Fix-It Parent will come in three weeks later and say, "That medication didn't work, my child still feels depressed."

Then I will have to explain again to them, "That's going to be the case with every medication we try. It's going to feel like it doesn't work at the two week mark, when in reality it is working."

It's difficult, but parents need to be patient if they want to help their child. When parents cannot be patient, the cost to the child is high. When parents take control of medicating their child and squeeze the psychiatrist out of the equation, their child often does not get better. They continue to suffer.

The goal is full resolution of a child's depressive symptoms, which is absolutely possible. Meeting that goal often requires medication to target resolving the biological symptoms. The SSRIs are only about 60 percent effective at resolving biological symptoms; the other 40 percent comes from therapy. Therapy and medication used in conjunction can lead to a 100 percent resolution of depressive symptoms. This entire process takes about a year. With medication, you can get 60 percent better in about six months. Without medication, you get to the 60 percent point in one year. Medication often shortens the time of depression from one year to six months.

During the one year of taking an antidepressant every day, the cells in the brain are bathed in a consistent level of serotonin. This is important because the cells of the human body naturally maintain "homeostasis," which is basically a constant or stable environment for the cell to live in. After a year, the new homeostasis becomes the standard, so that when the medication is slowly taken away, the cells react by trying to maintain the new higher level of serotonin. The cells in effect are conditioned and stimulated to increase the amount of serotonin made and available to brain cells. This process helps prevent depression from recurring.

When parents make a commitment to work in conjunction with their psychiatrist, they become a Healer Parent. The Healer Parent, first and foremost, partners with the psychiatrist. They monitor the medication, express their expectations and disappointments, ask questions, share their concerns about the medications, and commit to the process required to discover the correct dose. In some cases, we might need to change the time of day that the child takes the medication, because they are struggling with insomnia. We may need to change from taking the medication in the morning to taking it at bedtime. We may need to split a dose because a child's metabolism is very fast. Often, much fine tuning is needed to discover what works for a child. The Healer Parent is committed to this process.

I hear from many patients that they don't want to feel like they're being used as a "guinea pig" in an experiment. It's not that psychiatrists are experimenting, it's that we have to be flexible in how we use the medication to meet individual needs as determined by their unique biology, psychology, and lifestyle.

Treatment for anxiety differs from treatment for depression in a couple of significant ways. Treating anxiety often requires higher doses of an antidepressant. Anxiety requires a therapeutic intervention in addition to medication so a person can learn skills to manage their anxiety. Unlike depression, we don't want our anxiety to be 100 percent resolved, because anxiety is actually good for us. We need anxiety to live; it's what motivates us to do things, to accomplish goals, and to take care of ourselves. The goal in treating anxiety is to get the anxiety to a point where it's reasonable, rational, and manageable. It's hard to nail down an exact time frame for healing anxiety. There are different kinds of anxiety disorders, such as generalized anxiety, social anxiety, and obsessive compulsive disorder (which requires specialized treatments). When treating anxiety, the patient may need different medications in addition to antidepressants. There are multiple strategies for treatment depending on individual needs.

In the treatment of social anxiety and generalized anxiety, moderate doses of an antidepressant, such as Prozac, Zoloft, Lexapro, Trintellix, Effexor, Remeron, or Cymbalta, may work well to reduce anxiety. These medications coupled with cognitive behavioral therapy can be effective in helping children begin to endure the school or classroom setting, and accomplish daily goals without second-guessing themselves too much. On the other hand, for disorders such as obsessive compulsive disorder (OCD), much higher dosages of an antidepressant are necessary to lessen anxiety. In addition, medications to augment or enhance the action of the antidepressants, or medications to target other neurological receptors (such as dopamine receptors) may also be necessary.

CHAPTER 4

Nutrition

The emerging study of nutrition's role in mental health offers encouraging possibilities for those dealing with mental illness. Many simple nutrition interventions show promise for helping people better manage anxiety and depression. As we learn more about how nutrition affects mental health, both parents and children can experience the empowerment that comes with playing a significant role in their healing process. Nutrition is an area that leaves it up to parents to make decisions and follow through with the dietary changes that promote healing.

Preventative medicine has been an important focus in the field of medicine but prevention strategies are just now beginning to be understood and used in mental health. There are many simple nutritional changes we can make regarding what we feed our children that might reduce the severity of mental illness. When parents commit to being a Healer Parent from the beginning of a child's life, they go a long way toward reducing or preventing some symptoms of mental illness. The genetic factors influencing mental illness cannot be changed; however, they can certainly be mitigated when we teach our children how to take care of their bodies and minds.

Research has shown that people who suffer from depression and anxiety often have poor diets. Specifically, the worst diets for mental illness are those high in fatty foods, sugar, and carbohydrates, and low in fruits, vegetables, leafy greens, and proteins.

SUGAR

More parents are beginning to identify a link between when their child takes in sugar and when they don't. Scientists are beginning to notice a difference too. There is a large body of preliminary evidence that supports the idea that increased sugar consumption is linked to depression and anxiety. It is worthwhile for us to consider how limiting sugar in our children's diets might help reduce depressive and anxious symptoms.

Toward the end of the initial evaluation as I sit with parents and their child, parents ask me, "What do you think about all the sugar my child eats? We feel it is just too much, and it seems like it affects her mood."

These parents are right. In studies completed around the world, researchers are noticing that children who eat junk food (foods with high levels of carbohydrates, fats, and sugars, which have low nutritional value) and high-sugar foods (like soda and candy), have more symptoms of depression and anxiety.

These children do not necessarily have enough severity of symptoms to meet criteria for the diagnosis of a clinical depression or an anxiety disorder, but they do have significant levels of depressive or anxious symptoms. This means that even children without depression or anxiety will have symptoms that look like they are depressed and anxious if they are eating foods with little nutritious content and high sugar and carbohydrate content.

When tweens without depression and anxiety take in too much sugar, they will have many of the following symptoms: sleeplessness, irritability, moodiness, sadness, hopelessness, crying spells, low frustration tolerance, an increase in acting out, changes in appetite, low energy, lack of interest in usual activities, low self-esteem, increased nervousness, and worries. These are the same symptoms that children who struggle with a clinical depression or anxiety disorder have.

Many years ago I took care of a young tween, a boy of eight years old. He was diagnosed with a depressive disorder, and had been stable for a few months. However, for his birthday, he had several birthday parties, and ate only birthday sweets, such as birthday cake, ice cream, cookies, and soda. His mother described him as becoming hyperactive, irritable, and moody. His behavior escalated throughout the day, and by the time it was bedtime, he was in a full-blown tantrum. His parents had to take him to the hospital, and he stayed for two days before he was calm enough to go home. This is an extreme example, but illustrates how even when stable on medications for several months, one day of sugary foods was enough to make him unable to regulate his mood and behavior.

What is the correct amount of sugar that a child can have? How do parents limit their child's intake of sugar? There are no established guidelines to specify amounts of sugar, only the recommendation to increase the nutrition content of the foods that children eat. Clearly a day of candy, sweets, soda, and cake is too much. I encourage parents to use their best judgement, and if you notice that your child becomes moody, irritable, sad, or unable to regulate themselves, then note that they may have had too much sugar or carbohydrates that day. A diet rich in vegetables and fruits is healthier than a diet with processed foods. Even processed foods with one serving of fruit, such as the gummy fruit drops that children seem to enjoy, have too much sugar. Any foods that are processed take foods that are made of complex sugars and change them to simple sugars. Eating those gummy fruit drops is the same as eating handfuls of candy. A baggie of blueberries is just as sweet, but much more nutritious (with complex sugars, fiber, and vitamins) and less likely to negatively impact your child's mental health.

CARBOHYDRATES

Many fad diets promote very low or no carbohydrates in the diet. This elimination of all carbohydrates is actually not healthy for the brain. Not all carbohydrates are unhealthy. In fact, carbohydrates support the healing of depression. However, the carbohydrates that support healing are those with a low glycemic index. In other words, carbohydrates that release glucose into the bloodstream slowly. The carbohydrates that are good for depression include: some fruits, vegetables, whole grains, and whole grain pasta. The carbohydrates that have a high glycemic index include sweets, candy, and desserts. Eating carbohydrates triggers the release of insulin. Insulin is the chemical our body produces that allows for sugar to enter a cell so that it can be used for energy. At the same time, insulin allows for a protein called tryptophan to enter the neuron. Tryptophan enters cells in the brain and it can be used to make serotonin. Serotonin is a neurotransmitter which helps anyone feel good and specifically helps with depression.

The carbohydrates that people struggling with anxiety and depression should avoid include processed wheat, white bread, pasta (other than whole grain), processed cereals, candy, cookies, and all junk food. Also, anything processed, including premade foods that are found in the freezer section of a grocery store, should be avoided. Those carbohydrates are so highly processed that it's practically the same as sugar going straight into your bloodstream. They look like whole carbohydrates, but really they are simple sugars marketed to look complex.

DAMAGING DRINKS

When it comes to drinks, anything that contains simple sugars like high-fructose corn syrup, sugar, or even fruit juice provides a big shot of harmful simple sugars to the bloodstream and therefore should be avoided. The healthiest drink, especially for anyone struggling with mental illness, is water. Many parents complain to me about how much soda their child drinks. It can be challenging to get a tween to give up their high-glycemic drink of choice. Prevention is the best option for heading off dependence on sugary drinks. During a child's infancy, as a child is weaned off of formula or breast milk, I recommend that parents skip offering soda or fruit drinks to toddlers. Instead, I recommend that parents offer water as the only clear liquid option, so that children will grow up with the healthy habit of drinking water.

I have a patient in his early twenties who struggles with autism.

One of the most challenging power struggles that his parents and I face is his attachment to soda. He loves soda, but when he drinks it his mood becomes so dysregulated that he makes unsafe decisions like starting fires in his room or getting into verbal altercations and fights with peers and other adults. On several occasions, this has led to peers lashing out at him physically. His post-soda moods often make him unable to complete his work, which jeopardizes his employment and his living situation. All this occurs from drinking just two sixteen-ounce sodas. When this young man is not drinking soda, his behavior is pleasant and jovial and he displays good judgment. Almost every difficult day he has experienced coincides with drinking soda.

I do believe that children can be educated at a young age about their nutrition. Parents can start educating their kids early on about unhealthy versus healthy carbohydrates and other benefits of healthy eating. Discussions about nutrition ideally would start when kids begin to eat table food. Healthy eating can be modeled for children by parents making healthy choices in their own diets. Children are always watching us. We can take full advantage of that by making healthy choices ourselves in addition to educating them. For example, when children ask for unhealthy carbohydrates, we can point out to them how manufacturers are skilled at attracting children to desire unhealthy food. It's important not to just say "no, you can't have that," or bounce to the other extreme of giving in and buying what our child wants.

The healthy practice is to get in the habit of telling kids, "No, that's not good for you and I don't want you to eat unhealthy foods. We're not going to choose that, but let's get something that's better for all of us, something that tastes delicious and will keep us healthy."

When we get into the habit of using those words at a very young age, it becomes a part of the child's inner dialogue.

Other ways to develop our children's awareness about nutrition is to ask them when they ask for something to eat, "Do you think that's good for you?"

Depending on what they say, you can respond with information.

"I know it looks attractive and fun, but it's actually not healthy for you. The food manufacturers make their products sound and look healthy to you, but many are not. I know it looks really good and easy to eat, but it's just as easy and tasty to eat a strawberry. It leaves less trash for the environment and it's much healthier for our bodies and minds."

This kind of conversation will also support what kids are learning in school. Kids are being taught about the environment, conservation, and recycling. Parents can build on what's happening at school and help them make choices that are in line with what they are learning. Children from the ages of eight to twelve want to do what's right and good. They are highly motivated to do the right thing by following the rules. This is a prime time for parents to teach their child how to make healthy choices for themselves, for their well-being, and for the health of our planet.

PROTEIN

Protein-rich foods are made up of amino acids which are used by the body to manufacture the proteins essential for producing neurotransmitters, other essential chemicals, cellular structures, energy, and more. Our bodies make twelve amino acids; we need to take in the other eight from the food we eat. Healthy diets include proteins with the eight essential amino acids our body cannot produce. Foods with protein and essential amino acids include beets, milk, eggs, beans, peas, and grains. Serotonin and dopamine are made up of two essential amino acids, tyrosine and tryptophan. When our bodies lack those two amino acids, we cannot produce sufficient amounts of dopamine and serotonin. This can lead to depression and anxiety.

Tyrosine is found in meats and tryptophan is found in carbohydrates like whole grains. Low levels of serotonin in the brain have been associated with low mood and aggression. At the other extreme, a diet too rich in proteins can lead to a buildup of amino acids and cause brain damage and mental retardation. When we take in more protein than our body can metabolize, the excess is stored in cells and that causes a buildup. In the genetic illness phenylketonuria (PKU), children lack the gene that breaks down phenylalanine, causing a buildup of amino acids that leads to brain damage and mental retardation. For kids who want a strictly vegan diet, parents need to look carefully at the foods their children are willing to eat and make sure that the eight essential amino acids occur in sufficient amounts. Amino acid supplements may be necessary.

ESSENTIAL FATTY ACIDS

Any discussion about mental health and well-being must take into consideration the needs of the brain. Our brains make everything happen in the body. When we take care of our brain we take care of the rest of us, including our thinking, our mood, and how our bodies function. Our brain consists mostly of fat, or lipids, so we need to take in certain fats in our diet to promote a healthy brain structure. Omega-3 fatty acids, in particular, are extremely important for the brain as they make up about a third of the fatty acids in our brains. There are studies showing that people struggling with depression have decreased levels of omega-3 fatty acids in the brain and the bloodstream.

Omega-6 fatty acids are also important for brain health. Fatty acids contribute to the integrity of the nerve cells in the brain, which in turn contributes to the functioning of the nerve cells. For years physicians have recommended that people increase their intake of both omega-3 and omega-6 fatty acids to help improve mood; this works for depression and bipolar disorder. There are some studies suggesting that upping our intake of these fatty acids can help with dyslexia and autism.

You can get your omegas through both foods and supplements. There are omega supplements that derive their fatty acids from algae for those who are vegan or vegetarian. Foods high in omegas include: soy milk, salmon (skin and roe), sardines, some dairy products, eggs, chia seeds, hemp seeds, flax seeds, anchovies, sardines, herring, mackerel, and a Japanese food called nattō derived from soybeans. You can also buy foods fortified with omegas including eggs, peanut butter, and some cereals. The best sources, however, are seafood.

VITAMINS

A recent study indicates that vitamin supplementation for one year improves mood for both men and women. The most important vitamins include the B complex vitamins like vitamin B12, Folate, vitamin B2, and vitamin B6. These are important for sustaining, maintaining, and improving mood. Thiamine is a B vitamin that helps with cognitive performance, brain functioning, and intellectual abilities. Vitamin B12 helps with brain development. During the preadolescent and adolescent years it's important to support brain development as much as possible. Research has shown that people diagnosed with depression had folate levels 25 percent lower than people who didn't have depression. It's also been shown that if folate levels are low, antidepressants will not work as well. Folate is used to produce serotonin. If you have a diet low in folate, your brain does not have enough of this B vitamin to make the serotonin needed to enhance mood.

METHYLFOLATE

Up to forty percent of people in the United States have a mutation in the MTHFR gene to produce a protein on the cell's surface that transports folate from the bloodstream into the cell. The mutation makes the protein unable to bring folate into the cell. When a cell can't take in nutrients or elements directly, they employ proteins on their surface to help an element enter the cell. In some people diagnosed with depression, that transporter on the cell surface does not work well to transport folate into the brain cell. Even though someone might take in enough folate in their diet or through supplements, their brain can't actually utilize it fully because it doesn't have the transporter to get it into the cell. In these cases, genetic testing can be very helpful and should be considered when someone is not responding to antidepressant therapy—especially when their diet is rich in folate, proteins, fatty acids, and minerals that are important for mental health. Genetic testing is the best way to identify whether or not someone has the gene to make this important transporter. If someone has a mutation on the gene, they may require additional supplementation with methylfolate. This supplement has the methyl piece already on the folate so it can go into the cell, bypassing the need for that abnormal transporter. This is important for parents to become aware of. If their child with depression is getting enough folate and is still not responding to antidepressants, parents need to ask their medical provider about whether they should have methylfolate supplementation, which may require a prescription.

MINERALS

CALCIUM   Calcium is important to understand, because the selective serotonin reuptake inhibitors (SSRIs) like Prozac, Zoloft, Lexapro, and Celexa slow down or stop the absorption of calcium into bone. Taking SSRIs without calcium supplementation results in an increased risk of fractures. A child's bones are softer than adult bones. However, younger people are often more involved in sports and risk-taking, making them more prone to fractures than adults.

CHROMIUM   Chromium is another important trace mineral. Several studies have linked depression with low levels of chromium. For that reason, parents should make sure that any multivitamin given to their child contains chromium.

IODINE   Iodine is another very important trace mineral. It supports thyroid function. Any fluctuation in thyroid hormones can cause depression or anxiety. Thyroid hormones also support energy use in the brain cells. The top three sources of iodine include dried seaweed, codfish, and yogurt. Iodine is also found in turkey breast, navy beans, tuna, eggs, baked potato, cranberries, and strawberries.

LITHIUM   Lithium is both a trace mineral and a medicine that has been used in psychiatry since before the 1950s. It is the drug of choice for the treatment of bipolar disorder. It is an antidepressant with anti-suicidal properties. As a medication, lithium is one of only two medicines that has evidence for the prevention of suicide. Lithium decreases aggression, improves impulse control, and assists with eating disorders. It is an all-around mood stabilizer. Lithium is a medicine, but it is also an element. It can be found in foods such as shrimp, lobster, scallops, dairy, eggs, other meats, soft cheeses, herring, mushrooms, red cabbage, cucumber, asparagus, white cabbage, potatoes, apples, black tea, paprika, marjoram, cinnamon, instant soup, tomatoes, and, sometimes, tap water.

SELENIUM. Low levels of selenium have been implicated in people who have depression. In addition, healthy levels of selenium has been shown to decrease anxiety. Foods rich in selenium include: Brazil nuts, yellowfin tuna, halibut (cooked), sardines, grass-fed beef, boneless turkey, beef liver, and chicken.

ZINC. At least five studies have shown that zinc levels are lower in people suffering with depression. It has been found that zinc supplementation can boost the effectiveness of an antidepressant. Zinc protects brain cells from potential damage caused by free radicals. The research isn't terribly robust around the effect of zinc supplementation for children and adolescents; however, it does show some difficulties with mental functions and behaviors in kids who have diets low or deficient in zinc. Foods rich in zinc include spinach, beef, shrimp, kidney beans, flax seeds, pumpkin seeds, oysters, and watermelon seeds.

The Healer Parent understands the importance of the cliché "we are what we eat." Even more importantly, they understand that when parents invest their time and energy in helping their child understand the importance of taking care of themselves, the rewards last a lifetime. The key in the treatment of depression and anxiety in children is a parent's intention and sustained effort to support healing. The Healer Parent is able to see their child in his or her totality rather than as simply a diagnosis needing to be fixed. They continue to be cognizant of their child's development spiritually, intellectually, and physically (including nutrition). They understand the importance of becoming conscious and deliberate about food choices.

We don't have to be perfect parents. We don't have to eat the right amount of anything, but the intention and practice of caring at a specific and focused level gives the child the experience of feeling valuable. This helps a child develop self-esteem, which is protective against the feelings of emptiness and self-loathing that lead kids to hurt themselves, use drugs or alcohol, or self-sabotage. The most practical way we can prevent children from going down a path of self-destruction is to create experiences of self-care and value.

CHAPTER 5

The Fix-It Parent

vs.

The Healer Parent

Exasperated, the parents of my young client recorded her meltdown for me to witness firsthand. The scene begins with her screaming at her parents. In short order, this eight-year old began to throw books and toys around her room, and then at her parents. When she saw them with phones in hand, she screamed, "Turn the camera off!"

When her parents would not oblige her, she ran down the hallway, from one room to another slamming doors. She finally ended up in the bathroom where she locked the door. At that point, her parents were noticeably distraught, and afraid she would harm herself. When they were able to unlock the door, they found their daughter on the floor sobbing.

Sadly, this scene is common for the many parents whose child struggles with anxiety or depression. Few things are as upsetting as watching your child spiral into an out-of-control rage or hysterical meltdown. Parents can feel utterly helpless not knowing what to do in those situations.

Frustrated and afraid, most parents I work with will try everything from intuitive parenting to tough love and everything in between. While understandable, not all styles are helpful (and sometimes can be damaging) to their child. I have come to label parents that practice these ineffective parenting styles as Fix-It Parents.

Parents try a multitude of parenting styles in response to their child's mental health challenges:

Tiger mom: strict or demanding parents who push their children to success through achievement to the child's detriment. *Coined by Yale law professor Amy Chua

Helicopter parent: a hovering parent who pays too-close attention to a child's experiences and problems. *Coined by Foster Cline and Jim Fay

Freestyle parenting: in-the-moment parenting, no planning, no boundaries, and no continuity.

Authoritarian parenting: this parenting style is restrictive and punishment-heavy with no reasoning to the child for the parent's actions.

The pain of watching a child struggle with a mental illness motivates many parents to want to "fix" their child or the situation so that the child does not have to struggle anymore. Unfortunately, this well-intentioned effort to fix often backfires, and leads to both parent and child feeling disconnected and helpless. Learning to take a more healing approach not only helps parents and children feel closer to each other, but also helps the child more quickly heal their mood or anxiety disorders. Moving from being a Fix-It Parent to being a Healer Parent can make all the difference in a child's healing prognosis, not to mention improving family harmony. Gratefully, it's not difficult to learn.

When a child's upset escalates into screaming, crying, or

punching walls, parents have an opportunity to respond in a way that brings calm to their child and the situation, and even promotes their child's healing. I have come to refer to this helpful and informed parenting style as Healer Parenting. This more-effective strategy requires that parents learn how to be a Healer Parent by practicing these skills when their child is calm. It can take some time to make this way of interacting with your child a regular habit, but the effort is well worth it. Like a martial artist who enters the dojo to practice sequence after repetitive sequence of hits, blocks, and kicks to prepare for a tournament, parents can continually practice their healer skills to improve their daily interactions with their child. The skills that make everyday interactions go more smoothly are the very same skills that work to successfully intervene during a crisis. Not only will you, the parent, be confident and prepared, your child will recognize your intention to heal and soothe, and then become conditioned to respond positively to your interventions.

Liam was an intelligent eleven-year-old boy who refused to turn in his homework. His mother brought him to see me because he was in danger of being asked to leave his prestigious private school. She was at her wit's end. I evaluated Liam and found that he was struggling with a significant anxiety disorder that also triggered bouts of depression. Though he started medication to target the anxiety disorder, he continued to struggle with his behavior. The more his mother raised her voice and insisted that he turn in his homework, the less likely he was to take it out of his backpack. Liam's other concerning behaviors included yelling back at his mother and stepfather, destroying property at the home, and running away to his father's or grandmother's home.

Liam and I started therapy once a week, a mixture of play therapy and talk therapy. Not surprisingly, whenever we began to talk about anything of substance, he ran out of my office, and I would walk outside to find him fuming at the front of the building. I was able to coax him back into interacting with me by simply asking if he would like to play. I let him choose, and we mostly played outside. I let him direct our play for many months before he could tolerate playing and talking in my office.

Meanwhile, I spent time with his mother discussing how she could support his healing process. She learned to back off from asking him about his homework and requesting that he not behave poorly. Instead, she asked him how she could spend time with him. She learned how to give him her attention by following his lead. She began to enjoy her time with him, and he began to turn in his homework. He stopped breaking things in the home and he asked for permission before leaving the house to visit his father or grandmother. All of his concerning behaviors changed without anyone directly telling him to change them. These breakthroughs happened after I taught mom how to move from being a Fix-It Parent to a Healer Parent. With both of us on the same page, the changes happened quickly.

Moving from being a Fix-It Parent to being a Healer Parent is a process that anyone can do. It simply requires learning a few basic steps, and then understanding the ways in which change happens on a neurological, psychological, and behavioral level. Using the tools presented in upcoming chapters will ensure that Fix-It Parenting styles will be used less, and Healer Parenting styles will be easy and automatic to use.

TAKE A STEP BACK

When you step back, your child can step forward. While still a resident-level physician in the Bay Area of Northern California, I had the unique opportunity to care for Koko—the gorilla who became famous for learning sign language—and her companion, Ndume. Ndume was a beautiful male silverback western lowland gorilla with an anxiety disorder. He got frightened when anyone got close to him. When he was growing up as a baby in another zoo, the other gorillas threw things at him and harassed him. He developed a fear of other apes and people because of this mistreatment. When he became afraid, he regurgitated food into his hand and threw it at anyone who got too close. I wore a raincoat around him for a few months. Over time, Ndume began to trust me. This was evident to me in that he wouldn't immediately throw regurgitated food at me. He would hold it in his hand as he assessed the situation and gauged how close I was getting to him. We researchers all learned to take slow steps and build a relationship with him before approaching him. If you got too close, he would make the motion of regurgitating into his hand and then he would give a sideways look like, *Okay, that's too close.* When we took a step back, his whole body relaxed and he put his hand down, interacted with us, and even played clapping games. If we took steps toward him, he postured again. On the other hand, when he was in his home, he allowed me to get close enough to put a tortilla slathered with almond butter right into his mouth! He was in his safe place, and felt secure enough to be affectionate and inviting.

The gorillas taught me a lot about how to interact with anxious or depressed people. The gorillas are acutely aware of your body language, your voice, and your eye contact and will react immediately to perceived threats.

The lessons we can take from the gorillas? Pay close attention to changes in your child's behavior. When your child starts to fidget or cry or frown, take a step back. These are the signs of fight-or-flight responses and indicate that someone is about to escalate their stressed behaviors. When in a location that is familiar to them, a safe place, your child is more likely to feel secure and can more easily connect with you.

CREATE A PLACE TO CONNECT

When a child feels out of control, they need their parent to create a safe place for them to connect. This is best done before the child needs it. In interactions with upset children, it's helpful if parents remember that their child has depression or anxiety, which means they struggle intensely to regulate and manage their behavior and emotions. When parents keep this in mind, they are better able to anticipate which helpful strategies to use with their child before an episode. This involves designating a safe area to go to when the child begins to escalate. In my house, the place I go with my ten-year-old when he is having difficulties is his rocking chair.

When I see him starting to escalate I gently suggest, "Let's go to the rocking chair for a few minutes."

He usually agrees and we go sit together for ten or fifteen minutes, if he hasn't fully escalated. I don't say much, I just sit with him, and give him a hug when he leans into me. All these extensions of myself help him feel connected and safe. It's important that we start this practice early in a child's life and repeat often so that our child learns that there is a safe place readily available to calm down.

The parents of Bill, an eight year old boy, developed a ritual of taking a drive whenever Bill became anxious. They started this practice when he was an infant, because they discovered that he stopped crying whenever they drove around the block. They continued the practice even as a toddler, and realized that his body relaxed with the running of the engine. As Bill became aware of the ritual, he began to ask for it whenever he started to feel scared or unsure. During the car rides, Bill would take several minutes to regain his composure, but eventually he began to express his worries and share them with his parents. Bill's family incorporated the car ride ritual into road trips for family vacations. Their coping mechanism, through regular use, became a tradition enjoyed by the entire family.

I suggest to parents of my tween patients that they create this kind of ritual prior to a crisis so that the child knows both on a subconscious and conscious level that there is a tangible, reliable, safe place to go. On a psychological level, creating this kind of ritual is a form of classical conditioning. Similar to Pavlov's famous experiment that showed how dogs, through experiencing the same routine time and time again prior to getting dinner, start to salivate as they began to recognize sounds, sights, and smells that lead to them getting fed, children will also start to calm as soon as they unconsciously recognize their parents' attempts to lead them to a safe and soothing place. This connecting, calming place can be something very simple like a corner of the room, sitting on the bed together, or sitting on the couch. Find a place in the house that is easily accessible and reliable to get to. The idea is that this

61

will be a place where the child and the parent know they will have a connection between them.

COMMUNICATE, DON'T DIRECT

Once you designate a calming place, as your child starts to escalate, physically take a step back and lovingly intend, *Let's go calm down*. Make your words more of a suggestion than a directive, and suggest the act of connection.

Say things like, "Shall we go sit together in our spot?"

Express it in the terms of what you, the parent would like to do, not what the child needs to do.

Don't direct your child by saying commands such as, "You need to calm down. You need to come with me. You need to..."

Instead say, "I would like you to come with me, I would like to sit with you, I would like to give you a hug."

Be patient, as they will not likely take your suggestion right away. If they don't take your hand, then I recommend you physically walk away from your child and go to the safe place and wait.

Say, "I'm just going to wait over here and I would like you to join me when you are ready."

Stay and wait for them to come to you. Continue to breathe, knowing and trusting that this will work. Children desperately want to have a connection with their parent(s), but they may not have the ability to ask for or know they need it. With practice, they will come to you eventually.

One mother shared with me, "My daughter was having a tantrum so I asked if she wanted a hug and she said 'yes,' but I went to give her a hug and she pushed me away. I don't know what she wants."

Children don't know what they want so it's up to the parent to say, "I'm here waiting for you".

After extending an invitation, don't go do something else like going to the kitchen to make dinner or getting your phone out to text your friends. The first several times may take hours of waiting, but the investment of that time will pay off in the end because, in time, the child will begin to realize that their parent is always there for them. This realization occurs first on an unconscious level, then on a conscious, knowing level. Notably, it only occurs with the act of repetition.

PRACTICE, PRACTICE, PRACTICE

The repeated experience of sharing a calming place helps to create healthy pathways in your child's brain. This action will lead to them reacting to a stressful stimuli by seeking a calm place, instead of taking an anxious, defensive, out-of-control behavior and having a meltdown. This is the neurology behind Pavlov's classical conditioning theory. After weeks, and possibly even months, of practice, the child will get to the point of beginning to calm when they see the parent approach. Instead of getting defensive and escalating, the child will unconsciously come to expect that their parent will lead them to a place of safety and calmness, and will begin to feel soothed. The more parents practice these principles, the more habitual calming becomes, and the easier (and thus more enjoyable) parenting becomes.

Thinking they can control the process and the outcome of children, the Fix-It Parent believes that if they had a solution (such as the right medication, the right thing to say, or the right school), then their child's depression or anxiety would go away. This is simply not true and rarely works.

Below is a table listing the differences between the Fix-It Parent and Healer Parent. We all use both styles at different times to parent. When we learn to use more of the Healer Parenting style, it leads to more effective resolution of problematic behaviors; it decreases depression and reduces your child's anxiety.

FIX-IT PARENT VS. HEALER PARENT	
FIX-IT PARENT	**HEALER PARENT**
Denies and lies	Shares the truth
Is unpredictable	Is predictable
Minimizes	Recognizes the complexity of the disorder
Does not accept	Accepts
Focuses on misbehaviors	Focuses on the child's strengths
Speaks more than listens	Listens to understand
Loses patience	Trusts the child's ability to heal
Does not express expectations	Expresses expectations ahead of time
Overreacts	Stays calm
Has negative expectations	Anticipates success

DENIES AND LIES

Parents naturally resort to the defenses of denial and avoidance and then don't share their true feelings and concerns with their child. For instance, in families where there is financial or marital stress, parents do not tell their kids that they are struggling. While parents do not need to tell their children the details of the situation, their children feel the tension. If they do not know what is creating the tension, children often assume they are the cause of the stress.

A behavior that parents often do that becomes problematic is they fight or argue loudly enough for their kids to hear it.

Later when the kids say "I don't like to hear you guys fighting," the Fix-It Parent discounts the child's worries by saying "everything is fine," when it's not.

If children overhear a fight, parents need to gently share the truth with their kids.

"Yes, we got loud and were feeling upset. We were discussing something important to us, but it's not something for you to worry about."

They need to acknowledge to the child, "We should not have been yelling. That was too loud and it created tension and stress. Next time we will be careful to discuss our concerns somewhere else."

IS UNPREDICTABLE

Children crave structure and order, especially children between the ages of seven to twelve years old. Their cognitive development is primed for rules, learning, and methodology. Kids at this age often pay close attention to their parents' behaviors and how well their parents follow the rules.

An example is when the child corrects their parent for making a driving mistake by saying, "Mom, you forgot to turn on your turn signal."

Children at this age also become frustrated and even angry if plans for the day get changed. Likewise, if a parent is continually behaving in a way that is not consistent, children at this age find this difficult to handle. The Fix-It Parent expects the child to adapt and adjust without complaining. The child is not developmentally geared for that kind of flexibility. When depression or anxiety disorders are present, it is even more difficult for children to feel stable when the rules are not followed.

MINIMIZES

Fix-It Parents often minimize the impact of depression and anxiety. Believing they can control the process or the outcome of their child's struggle with anxiety and depression, the Fix-It Parent believes that if they say positive things, offer exciting experiences, or buy material luxuries they can effectively change their child's mood. They believe they can influence their behavior. However, while depression and anxiety are psychological ways of handling stress, they are also biological illnesses which arise from chemical imbalances. This means that both psychological factors and chemical factors play important roles in how depression and anxiety are treated and resolved. There are no easy answers on how to alleviate depression and anxiety. Medication alone will not do it, and therapy alone is also often not enough to fully pull a child out of a serious depression or anxiety disorder. Most significant mental disorders need a combination of treatments to fully help a child heal from depression or anxiety.

DOES NOT ACCEPT THE CHILD FOR ALL OF THEIR STRUGGLES AND STRENGTH

When Fix-It Parents get anxious about their child, they tend to get intrusive. Children with anxiety and depression often behave in ways that push their parents away. This makes it even more difficult for parents to know when they should let their child push them away and when they should approach their child. Parents need to find a balance between giving a child space, and being there in a nurturing and supportive way. Finding that balance can be difficult but it is essential for healing. One of the ways to find that balance is to keep notes, either on paper or in your head. Note when and why your child pushes you away. When you learn to understand the nuances in your child's mood and behavior, you can anticipate how your child is prone to react to a stressful situation, or note when a depression or anxiety attack might be beginning and intervene at that point. Children are much more receptive to a parent's intervention earlier rather than later. When they are already upset then "everything" tends to bother them.

FOCUSES ON ONLY THE MISBEHAVIORS OR DISPLEASING BEHAVIORS

The Fix-It Parent is on the lookout for opportunities to correct or improve their child's behavior and mood. They become very good at noticing the most subtle signs of irritability, anxiety, sadness, and anger. While the intent of parents is to be helpful, the outcome is that the child feels scrutinized and shamed.

The Healer Parent keeps their focus on the desired outcome and optimizes their child's strengths. The way to do this is to remind the child of their wants and brainstorm with them about how to achieve those goals. This includes asking the child how their behavior in the moment is reflecting who they are and what they want. For instance, if they are being rude to other family members, parents can take the child to their calming place and remind the child of how sweet, caring, and kind the child is.

Ask your child, "The way you were interacting with your sister... is that really how you want to be acting with her, or is there another way through your kindness, sweetness, and caring nature that you could express what you want from her?"

SPEAKS MORE THAN LISTENS

The Dalai Lama said, "When you talk, you are only repeating what you already know. But if you listen, you may learn something new."

Focusing on correcting a behavior, improving the mood, or dismissing anxiety causes parents to jump to conclusions and offer their child a solution too soon. If that solution is not applicable to the child's experience, the child will reject it, and display an unwanted behavior like becoming withdrawn or irritable, or acting out.

Instead of telling your child how to behave, the Healer Parent approaches the interaction with the intention to understand why the child is behaving the way they are. The Healer Parent can ask the child, "What's going on? What do you need? How can I help you?"

Give your child a few moments to respond. If they don't respond, ask them the same questions in an even gentler and softer tone. By listening to what the child needs first, the Healer Parent learns what interventions or actions they need to take to best help their child.

LOSES PATIENCE WITH THE CHILD OR THE HEALING PROCESS

It is difficult to tolerate even one day of a child who struggles with depression or anxiety. Impatience can lead to one of the biggest mistakes parents make in dealing with their anxious or depressed child: not partnering well with their child's providers, including the therapist and the psychiatric provider. Children with parents who develop a trusting relationship with their psychiatrist and therapist make progress faster. Many parents hold back from trusting the providers; they tinker with the medication or do just part of the treatment plan. They may seek outside resources, but don't tell the therapist or the psychiatrist. They hold information back so the therapist and psychiatrist make decisions based on half or less than half of the whole picture.

In those cases, both parties struggle to find out what's best for the child. This also puts the child in the middle. The child may trust the therapist and psychiatrist more than the parents do. Sometimes the parents trust the treatment team more than their child trusts the treatment team and that will also impact progress. Although the treatment process may be complex, the Healer Parent maintains trust in their child's ability to heal and their ability to work together with the treatment team. Understanding the healing process activates hope.

DOES NOT EXPRESS EXPECTATIONS AHEAD OF TIME

The best time to let children know how to behave appropriately is during non-crisis times, like during play or mundane activities. The most effective way to teach them is by your own example. While the Fix-It Parent reacts to misbehavior by pointing out mistakes and stating the appropriate behavior, the Healer Parent models good behavior every day by interacting with their child in the same way they expect the child to behave. Playing with toys, like figures and animals, is one way parents can display how people should speak to each other and how to react in unpleasant or disappointing situations.

Conversing about your expectations while driving to and from school and other activities is another time when children are open to hearing about what behavior is acceptable without feeling criticized. During these times, you can say things like, "Now we are going to go to the store to pick up some groceries, then go home. When we go to the grocery store, I need you to stay with me and help me choose groceries. Perhaps you could push the cart for me. I need you to push the cart slowly, at my pace, and stick right by me. When we go home, I will make dinner and I would like you to finish your homework. I can help you. I am looking forward to a nice dinner with you."

Though it may seem casual and understated, these mundane conversations can have a powerful influence on your child. When children are relaxed and secure they are able to receive information and reflect on more appropriate actions.

OVERREACTS

Depressed or anxious children are sensitive to excited reactions. When Fix-It Parents react with irritability, anger, disgust, or despair, their children feel shamed, defensive, and alone. Children may in turn react with even more aggression, defiance, or hysterics. If the parent continues to escalate and talk over the child in an effort to be heard, a pattern of one-upping each other ensues until both parent and child feel out of control and ineffective.

A more healing response would be to approach the child from a place of calm within yourself. When approaching the child with the intention to understand their experience of feeling upset, the child has no conscious or unconscious reason to escalate. That means they don't take a defensive posture and can be open to your assistance.

HAS NEGATIVE EXPECTATIONS

The Fix-It Parent expects that their child will misbehave and need redirection. They constantly wait for the other shoe to drop. This negative expectation not only sets a child up for failing to behave well, it also sets up an insecure interactive pattern between parent and child. This means that parents will be on the lookout for bad behavior and the child will be continually anxious about if they are behaving well or not. The enjoyment of spending time with each other gets lost in this kind of highly insecure interaction.

Children have an inherent desire to please their parents. Parents can use this powerful drive to motivate children to behave in safe and appropriate ways. When children know how to please their parents, they will make every attempt to do so. This means that if parents merely express to their child the behavior they want to experience, the child will behave in that way. When the child struggles with behaving in a pleasing way, parents can step in to assist.

When parents make statements like "I need you to do x, y, or z," then children know exactly what is expected of them.

If the child struggles with doing x, y, or z, then the parent can say, "I see that you are having some difficulty. What can I do to help?"

When the parent believes that the child can do it, the child internalizes that positive expectation and feels more self-confident.

Your awareness about the differences between the Fix-It Parent and Healer Parent can take you far when it comes to helping a child who struggles with anxiety or depression. If you recognize yourself in the description Fix-It Parent, I urge you to be gentle with yourself as you try on new behaviors. Once you are comfortable with the Healer Parent style, parenting the depressed or anxious child will be less stressful and more enjoyable.

Perfection is not the goal in parenting, but being good enough is. We can all be good enough parents when we have the knowledge and tools to be effective at helping our children develop through each stage of their young lives.

Even though the Fix-It Parent may seem like a more active parenting style, because they jump in to fix the problem, it's actually a passive parenting style. It's passive because it's a knee-jerk response based on reacting to feelings in the moment rather than choosing a strategy to maximize healing in the long run. The Fix-It Parent doesn't think about different ways to intervene. The Fix-It Parent thinks of how to solve the problem in the here and now. Often, it's an automatic response.

The Healer Parent is a more active parenting style. Even though the Healer Parent takes a step back, is calm, is gentle, is thoughtful, and these behaviors seem on the surface like the parent takes a passive stance, they don't. It's a very active, engaged way of parenting; it requires the

Healer Parent to think about multiple ways to intervene, consider the rationale for each intervention strategy, evaluate the possible outcomes, choose between the options, and then take action. The Healer Parent is not reactive, they are proactive to facilitate the healing process for their child.

When parents choose to take the Healer Parent stance, they give themselves and their children an opportunity to develop a deeper, more active, more joyful relationship. It's empowering for both parents and children when parents use the Healer rather than the Fixer style. In my practice, I observe that as depressive and anxious symptoms resolve for my young patients, the Healer Parents and their children don't need me as much. The more Healer skills parents acquire, our dynamic changes and they begin to use me less to write prescriptions, and more as a consultant in their healing journey. This is the ideal working therapeutic tripod.

CHAPTER 6

The Identified Patient

Often, when families first come into my office, the child is the identified patient. The child sits on the couch slumped down with their shoulders and head down, fidgeting, looking at the floor, legs shaking, looking like they want to crawl into a hole. The parents, by comparison, often have a lot of energy. They are leaning forward, sitting on the edge of their seat, and ready to tell me all the problems that they have with their child. After we have gone through the evaluation and I explain the dynamic, then the child looks more energetic. He sits up, looks around the room, and has newfound life and energy in his eyes. When I look over at the parents, they are often slumped in their chair and look a little heavier and solemn. While the energy initially shifts in the room, the goal of treatment remains to find balance for everyone in the family—and this is possible.

A balanced family dynamic happens when there is no need for any member of the family to take on the tension of another. In these families, there are no identified patients. As families draw upon their courage to face painful issues and work together to solve them, the family becomes more cohesive and harmonious. Finding this balance and harmony is possible no matter how challenging things might seem today.

Ethan, an eight-year-old boy diagnosed with ADHD, came to me for therapy. He was taking a stimulant medication and his parents didn't want me to change his prescription; they simply wanted me to do therapy. When I evaluated Ethan, I agreed he might have ADHD, but I also believed he had an anxiety disorder. At school he was disruptive, rough with the other kids, and oppositional with the teacher. He had a difficult time completing his tasks at school. At home, he was argumentative with his parents and unable to complete his homework assignments or get ready for school in the mornings. He was hyperactive and would often run away from his parents.

Soon after I completed his evaluation, we started play therapy. We sat on the floor with a lot of toys and built houses. He started with two different houses and added a third house. He explained that one was a friend's, one was his, and another was my house. He played out a dynamic where the main character of our play would go pick up a friend and play. They would often engage in high-energy activities like getting on skateboards or bicycles or in fast cars. Eventually they would end up at my play home where it was a little calmer. There they played calmer games and planted flowers in the garden. Over time, those calmer themes spread into his imaginary home as well. As I played with him over a period of months, his behavior at home and school calmed down. He became less oppositional and compulsive and could pay attention to his daily tasks, like getting ready for school. He also started to participate more with his family. I made no changes to his ADHD medication during the time I worked with him.

In the beginning, the parents focused on the problems they were having with their son. Over time, it became clear that the main problems were in their marriage. As part of family therapy, I met with Ethan's father and mother separately and together. His mother often presented significant anxiety and uncertainty. As Mom's anxiety about the marriage increased, her son's anxiety also increased. Ethan's mother also reported to me feeling isolated from her husband. When her husband talked to me alone, he shared that he had lost his job and was feeling emasculated. He also shared that he had started watching pornography. Over time, it became clear that he was struggling with sex and alcohol addictions. He went to treatment and both parents entered into marriage counseling after he completed his individual treatment. Both parents worked out their individual and couple's issues and, afterwards, their son improved dramatically. He stopped taking his ADHD medication and no longer needed to see me. Similar scenarios are common for children diagnosed with anxiety and depression.

A family structure consists of a unit of people who are emotionally bound to each other. The details of who is in the family are less important than the idea of the construct of a family unit. Children play a critical role no matter what the family structure: they act like shock absorbers for the tension that happens within the family unit.

If a problem or conflict does not get resolved between the adults, it will spill out onto the children, who feel it at a core level. Children may not know how to describe it or understand who or what is causing their uncomfortable feelings, but they feel all the tension in the family. They also feel joy in the family. They feel all the feelings that emerge from time to time within the family and they react to those feelings…*if* those feelings are not shared out in the open. For example, if there is a loss in the family, most will typically feel sad together and share in the feelings of grief. It's out in the open. When feelings and problems are shared, it rarely causes problems for a child. However, when parents experience marital conflict and have heated arguments and disagreements, the child feels all of this and internalizes the tension. This is an inevitable truth.

Some children are able to speak up to their parents and say, "Stop fighting, I can't take it," but most kids can't do that and they keep it inside.

Children rely on their caregivers to take care of them to provide safety, stability, security, food, shelter, and other basics of life. When that safety and stability gets threatened, as in the case of divorce, moving from one home to another, financial crisis, loss of a caregiver, or even a loss of a family pet, the child can begin to feel insecure. One of the ways that they unconsciously manage their insecurity is by getting depressed or anxious. Both of those states lead to behaviors that are destructive. The depressive reaction causes children to withdraw or become irritable. The anxiety reaction can cause children to focus that energy inward and excessively worry, or direct it outward by displaying behaviors such as aggression toward themselves and others.

When the child becomes the barometer for the health of the family, mental illness is a natural consequence. This happens when conflict in a family is ignored. It is not healthy for the family or the child. Children start acting out or become withdrawn and irritable. It's at this point when families bring children to me for professional help. There is hope with professional intervention; the family can learn to stop avoiding and start addressing issues directly, then the child no longer needs to be a barometer or shock absorber.

THE PARALLEL PROCESS

Parallel Process is a psychological term that describes why some behaviors and interactions occur. Almost always, the child's problems are a mirror image of a dynamic that is an issue somewhere else in the family. There exists the theory of the macro (big picture) and micro (a smaller part of the bigger picture). The micro always resembles the macro. How parents treat each other is replicated somewhere in the system. Whatever is happening within the child is happening somewhere else in the family and the child is just acting it out. When we understand this, then we can zoom out and look at not only the child but where the conflicts and issues are in the whole family. We can start to understand and heal the different areas of conflict and issues that are unresolved. This alleviates the child of carrying the burden of the whole family dynamic.

Most children I have worked with let out a huge sigh of relief when they learn that their issues are a reflection of other things going on in the family.

They say, "Yes, yes, that is what's happening!" after I explain the idea of the Parallel Process to the identified patient. All of a sudden the pressure that they had been feeling is now shared, and therefore lifted. Even ten- and eleven-year-olds can feel the pressure being shed and the accompanying sense of relief.

As soon as I become aware of a Parallel Process as part of the family dynamic, I share my observations with the child and the parents together in the same room. I don't share the details of the conflicts with the child, but I will say something similar to "there are conflicts in the family where the parents are not on the same page and that conflict creates a lot of tension for you, as the child in the family."

In order to help a child heal thoroughly, a therapist must understand a child's presenting problem while keeping in mind that the child is a part of the family structure and not separate. As I do the individual work to understand and address the issues of the child, I am continually looking at the family structure and paying attention to what is happening within the family dynamics. The child's behavior is not intended. It is something that happens below their level of conscious awareness. It happens because the child is particularly sensitive to the unspoken stresses of the family.

The term "acting out" is commonly used to describe problematic behaviors of children, tweens, and teenagers. It is also a common reason for parents to bring their children to see a therapist or psychiatric provider. While acting out is a generic, umbrella description of behavioral problems, it is also indicative that there is an underlying reason for the behavior. The acting out behavior is the behavioral manifestation or the representation of the Parallel Process. As we explore and discover which process within the family is being paralleled or acted out by the child, we can then direct treatment toward helping the family understand and address their issues, and help the child learn to behave in ways that are more indicative of his or her actual feelings, needs, and thoughts. The entire family will have an opportunity to heal when the Parallel Process is understood.

I reviewed a case with a trainee who was working with an eleven-year-old girl struggling with physical fights with adults and peers. The trainee wanted to put her into a day treatment program and start medication. I asked about the family; it sounded at first like they were attentive and interested in the child.

When I asked about what was going on between the parents, the trainee answered, "Actually, now that I remember, the mom is thinking about getting a divorce."

He shared with me that the parents' arguments would escalate into the mother and father screaming and throwing objects at each other. They did this in front of their child.

I said to him, "Now we know what's going on, and this child doesn't have an anxiety disorder. We have a child who is modeling the interactive style of her parents."

This is a classic Parallel Process in action. The child's behavior parallels the way the parents interact with each other.

Though everyone in a family is uniquely their own person, the family is a unit and behaves as one entity so that each part of the entity (each individual family member) affects every other part of the unit. It's similar to your physical body. When you injure one body part, it affects all the other parts. I recently injured the bottom of my big toe and started walking with pressure on the side of my foot to protect it. After walking this way for a couple of days, I threw off my whole foot structure and all my muscles tightened to the point where I could no longer bear weight on my foot. After that, my knee started hurting and then my hips. I healed quickly; however, this occurred because my practitioner deeply massaged my foot, and had me stop compensating by bearing weight on only the side of my foot to avoid my hurt toe. By addressing the pain directly, I was able to heal my whole foot, knee, and hip. It can be painful for family members to look at their own hurt, tease apart their issues, and allow for the pain to emerge. Only when the pain comes out can healing occur.

No family member brings a child to see a psychiatrist unless they care and love their child deeply. When parents become willing to allow a third person, a stranger, to come in and muck around in their family's issues to figure things out, they are at their wit's end. The psychiatric evaluation and treatment process is intrusive. I find that the families that come to me are ready to do whatever it takes.

Pain opens the door to healing. When my doctor dug in to manipulate and massage the fascia and muscles in my foot, it was very painful and a few times I had to ask her to back off. It's often the same in family therapy: we go in, and if it is too painful, a little too fast, or we bring out something that is so deep and defended, we need to back off and go more gently and figuratively massage that scar tissue.

Denial is the primary defense mechanism that grows to defend a person from feeling too much psychological or emotional pain, but in order to heal and move on from that pain, the denial needs to be teased apart and broken down. In order to heal, it takes work, and that means it requires developing the ability to tolerate pain. It also takes support. This kind of deep work has to be done in a supportive therapeutic environment. The instinct can be to throw off the blankets to uncover everything and start to point fingers and blame others, but I discourage this behavior. I want parents and children to realize how interconnected they are. It's not about blaming the parents for the child's behavior, but about understanding each person's vulnerabilities and the defenses their psyches have created to protect themselves. As part of the work done in therapy, each person will need to ask themselves if they need to keep those defenses or if they want to build new (healthier) defenses that allow for protection and interconnectedness between family members. That is the essence of moving through pain and painful experiences to enhance relationships within a family.

Samantha, a thirteen-year-old girl, presented herself as a perfectionist and was highly stressed by many situations in her life. Her parents were worried that she was restricting, binging, and purging her food. Her parents essentially came to me saying, "Please fix my daughter's eating disorder." Often in these cases, as I get to know the child better and work with the family, I find that someone else in the family has an eating disorder also, often the mother. With this knowledge, we then address the mother's history of struggling with an eating disorder, and how the mother's experience replays in the daughter.

As we dove in deeply with Samantha and her mother, we

uncovered a history of molestation and trauma. First, Samantha shared with me her experience and later her mom shared that she had the same history of abuse. In fact, the same person in the family molested both of them. I worked with both the child and her mother to address their issues around trauma to begin healing their eating disorders. It took a few years, but they did eventually heal. Samantha's mother's willingness to look at and heal her issues facilitated her daughter's healing. In this case, Samantha was the identified patient; when the family was able to address the secret trauma in the family, the entire family unit was strengthened.

A projection is an unconscious defense mechanism, in which an individual "throws" their own internal, unresolved, conflicted feelings onto another person—often onto the ones we love the most. We need to resolve these underlying conflicts in order to be in control of our actions, thoughts, and words and to create the lives we want. The targets of our projections are often the people who try to be empathetic with us. Empathy is like a conduit for these projections. Our family members are the people we are closest to in our lives. The bonds formed between family members happen at a deep level. When we bond at that deep level, and encounter conflicts, our psyche accesses primitive and unconscious defenses that we are not even aware of. Most people don't realize they are projecting a deep-seated problem of their own onto their child.

If a parent has had a painful loss in their lives that was too much for them to fully process and grieve, they carry around that grief in their subconscious mind. Jane, a thirty-three-year-old mother, miscarried her second pregnancy. The defense mechanism of unresolved grief is to avoid anything that reminds them about the original cause of grief. For Jane, having a child who is quite empathetic and sensitive can be triggering. Jane's child, Lisa, became very sad about the death of their hamster. Jane became overly anxious and critical of Lisa's expression of sadness because it made her unconsciously uncomfortable about her own unresolved grief over her miscarriage.

Jane became tense and terse and even yelled at Lisa, saying, "It's just a hamster. Get over it."

Often, parents aren't able to show understanding for their child's expression of sadness because unconsciously they can't endure the child's grief. The message the child gets is, *I should be afraid of my sadness. I can't be sad.* This is anxiety-provoking for the child. If Jane had processed her own grief, she would be better able to handle her child's normal and natural reaction to her hamster dying.

One of the goals of family therapy is to begin to see how each family member's subconscious, unresolved conflicts are played out within the family dynamic. As the therapist brings more awareness to the family about their unconscious conflicts, and how they're being projected onto another person, the family members have a chance to own their own feelings and take responsibility for their previously unknown conflicts. Only then can the projections start to wane. When each person starts to realize who they are as individuals within the family, they can make new choices and learn how to function in a way that makes the family stronger. They can learn how to support each other and also receive support from other family members, sometimes for the first time.

When we have a life experience that we find challenging or confusing, an experience that generated feelings inside of us that were too difficult to handle in the moment, our psyches develop defense mechanisms to protect us from these emotions that are too hard to handle. Our psyche uses these defense mechanisms to bury our feelings because we simply don't know how to deal with it. That works for us in many situations. Most of us experience these feelings that we don't know anything about. We forget about it and ignore the feelings that are difficult to face. The problem with this strategy is that because we avoid it and don't think about it, we aren't consciously aware of what we have buried inside of us. Sometimes these feelings come out later in ways that we cannot control.

Most anxious responses in children happen as a result of

projections from close family members. An eleven-year-old little girl came to my office distraught and having panic attacks multiple times per day. I discovered that her parents were never on the same page and contemplating separating. She could not make decisions and was constantly having panic attacks because she held all of their uncertainty and internalized their conflict.

When I spoke to the parents, their demeanor was very calm, even though they had many conflicts. When I sat with them, I held all of their anxiety for about twenty minutes so I could get a feel for what their daughter was experiencing. This child's parents were projecting all their ambivalence and their deep resentment and hurt feelings about each other onto their daughter. The child acted out their ambivalence in the form of panic attacks whenever she was presented with a decision.

A deeper look into this family revealed that while this child's parents were deeply in love with each other, they both had betrayed each other, and both were hurt and angry about those betrayals. They were angry at themselves and angry with each other. They felt guilty and had no idea how to get back on the same page. They had the same temperament: a combination of being intense and sensitive.

Once I understood what was going on, I asked the child to leave the room. I laid it out on the table for them, gently. I explained how I was having a hard time understanding what the two of them as a couple wanted to do.

They said, "We want our daughter to stop having panic attacks and being so anxious."

I responded, "I understand that. I'm asking what you want to do about your marriage."

They fell silent. After a few moments, they said, "We want to stay together."

I said, "Okay, if you want to stay together, then you need to work on your relationship."

Then they both interrupted with blame and accusations. "He does this…" "She does that…"

I interrupted them, "This is a big part of the problem. You are blaming each other for disagreements and disappointments in your marriage, which is understandable. But you need to work through your problems if you want to help your daughter, and there are no quick fixes. I can't just tell you not to talk to your spouse like that. I would like to be able to tell you what to do and have it happen, but you need to understand your feelings. You need the opportunity to air those hurt feelings and learn to understand each other better. There also needs to be a process of practicing forgiveness. Then you need to start to forget and move forward. I think once you begin that process, your child's anxiety will plummet. When the two of you start to take responsibility for resolving your issues, your daughter can get back to the happy little girl she used to be. She won't have to unconsciously or consciously worry about what's going on between the two of you."

After I gave them that information, they agreed and then disclosed that they had heard the same thing from about five other psychiatrists and therapists. The parents were more interested in having their daughter fixed than taking responsibility for contributing to her problems—classic Fix-It Parenting. Unfortunately, their daughter started to call me every day, six or seven times a day, in a panic and the parents didn't know what to do. Eventually they left my practice. I suspect they went on to repeat the same cycle with a new therapist or psychiatrist. When parents are able to understand the dynamic, accept that it's not a quick fix, and commit at least a year, they can heal their projections.

In healthy families, children do not act as shock absorbers for the conflict in the family. Healthy parents are proactive and upfront with each other about their issues, their feelings, and their experiences. When a conflict arises between these parents, they deal with it. If the problem becomes overwhelming, the parents get assistance from therapists, friends, or spiritual leaders. They do not allow the conflict to fester and grow. Healthy parents also treat each other with respect, compassion, and kindness no matter what challenges they face.

How parents treat each other is reflected in how the child feels about him/herself. If the parents are respectful, accepting, patient, compassionate, forgiving, and tolerant, the child will feel the same way about themselves.

Marital conflict is one of the most common projected Parallel Processes. Jonathan was a twelve-year-old boy who was not turning in his homework, feeling withdrawn, and frequently retreating to his room. He started smoking marijuana, staying out late, and talking back to his parents and teachers. He was not completing his chores and his parents felt exasperated. They were scared that he was getting depressed and using drugs, and did not know what to do. He was irritable and oppositional, and denied everything his parents said about him when the four of us were together.

When the parents left the room, he told me, "I just can't stand my home. There's so much stress there. I can't take it."

I asked him what the stress was and he said it was so overwhelming to him that he couldn't pinpoint it. As it turns out, the issue was his parents' marital conflict, but he could not name it.

All he could say was, "It's just horrible. I hate it. They are always yelling and they're always on my case. I hate it there. I have to go."

This is the stance many kids in these circumstances take. They basically bide their time until they can leave the home (and go to college, live with another family member or friend, or set out on their own). In the meantime they withdraw their energy from school, so their grades drop. They start interacting with peer groups that may not be healthy for them. They start to use substances and go down an unhealthy path riddled with bad choices. They do all of this in an effort to not feel the stress at home. If they have a genetic or family history of mood or anxiety disorders, they are even more prone to becoming clinically depressed or anxious. This sets up the perfect storm for children to go down an unhealthy path that can lead to self-harm or even suicide.

They feel that they are in a helpless position because they believe there is nothing they can do to alleviate the stress coming from within the family.

When Jonathan went to the waiting room and I spoke to his parents alone, I asked them, "What is going on in the home? What are the stressors? What is going on between the two of you?"

As is often the case, Jonathan's parents were honest, open, and ready to be vulnerable. It was a relief for both of them to share their struggle.

They shared, "We have been fighting a lot and concerned about our finances. Oftentimes the exchanges get heated."

There in the office, their exchanges did get heated and I got to see, feel, and experience what it was like for their child. I appreciated seeing their true interactive style, because then we could start to intervene and make progress. As the parents' tension, anxiety, and fear escalated, I found myself worrying, *My goodness, I don't know where this is going to go.* In those cases, I know that the child must feel even more stressed.

I have an advantage that children in the same situation do not have. I have decades of training and experience to know how to handle the intense feelings that arise in me. I know not to take on another's feelings, whereas a child does not. This kind of experience with parents authentically expressing themselves can be a powerful tool for me to start to understand what the child is feeling. Afterwards, I can relate my experience back to the parents. I will let the parents know what it feels like to be in their child's shoes.

I will say something like, "I can feel the stress between the two of you, it makes my chest feel tight. If I'm feeling like this, imagine what your child feels every time they experience this tension between you."

In Jonathan's case, I shared with his parents, "There is a lot of conflict here. I know there's a lot of love here too, and that you are committed to healing."

The light bulb often turns on at this point, and parents are open to changing their interactions. Once they recognize how their aggression toward each other affects their child, they are more open to assistance.

I help them understand their strengths, their commitment, and their ability to be vulnerable. From that place, they are able to learn how to interact in a way that is true to their inherent compassion.

CHAPTER 7

Starting Therapy

When depression or anxiety is serious and the accompanying behaviors are significant, meaningful change takes time, usually a year or more. When children who do not have a significant impairment, like anxiety or depression, go through a challenging situation—like the loss of a family pet, or a move to a new home—they may just need a couple of months of support to adjust to the new changes.

It takes time to build a relationship and establish trust between the therapist and the child…for a child to like someone and feel understood. Though it may seem frivolous, this relationship-building phase is necessary in order for healing to take place. Without a relationship between the therapist and the patient, a child's healing will be inadequate. Parents often want to see results quickly and that is understandable. They are dealing with challenging behaviors on a daily basis and it is very painful to see their child struggle. Strong groundwork must be laid for lasting change to occur.

Yuri was a sweet eleven-year-old boy with a polite demeanor and a soft-spoken voice. While in my office, he would often quietly sit and play with toys. He was good at connecting with people and made eye contact when he spoke to me. He was generally thoughtful and considerate. At home, Yuri displayed a different side. His mother reported that he would fly into a rage if he heard something he did not like. If his parents requested something simple like asking him to go upstairs and go to bed, he would throw a tantrum.

During his tantrums, he would hit his brother, run up and down the stairs, kick wildly, or throw his body on the floor. His tantrums were more like those of a five-year-old rather than an eleven-year-old.

He would cry and yell at his parents, "I hate you," and then say, "I hate myself!"

The only thing that seemed to calm him was his dad holding him tightly in a bear hug for at least half an hour. After that physical, yet loving, containment he would go to his room, sleep for two hours, and come back ready to be polite again.

I evaluated Yuri and concluded that he struggled with a high level of anxiety and some depression. He was self-conscious, scared, and unsure about how to express his feelings about most things of importance to him: school, friends, or himself. He presented as more feminine than a typical eleven-year-old boy. He liked to paint his nails and carry purses. As a result of this, he was bullied at school. Happily, his family was extremely open and tolerant; they simply wanted to support his growth and self-confidence. We started a low dose of antidepressant medication to help him with his anxiety. We also started a medication to help him with impulsivity. He had been raging every day when I first started seeing him. The medicine helped calm the excitability in his brain that led to the raging behavior. I also recommended that he start therapy.

"It's going really well, I like my therapist," he reported. "She is fun and we talk about lots of things."

Yuri's mom reported to me he did indeed seem to like his therapist, but she also expressed concern. "He is still angry, irritable, and raging and we don't understand what's going on in therapy. It seems that all they do is play games. Should we continue?"

I said, "Yes, absolutely keep seeing her, because the first several months are about him making a connection and forming a therapeutic relationship with his therapist, and not so much about him making changes in his behavior."

His mom said, "All right we'll try to be patient, but it's hard when nothing much has changed."

I explained, "Therapy is something I like to plan on for a year. We need to be patient and wait for the therapy to do its magic. I assure you, a year from now things will be different. You can realistically expect to see significant changes in six months and major changes in a year."

This fact often surprises many parents who expect to see significant results after a few months of therapy.

Sure enough, about six months later Yuri's rages went from one or two a day to one or two per month and they were short-lived. He was able to accept his dad's bear hugs easily, and it took him only about thirty seconds instead of thirty minutes to calm down. A year later, the rages had completely ceased and he was a happy, well-adjusted boy. Yuri was also able to understand and talk about why he felt angry. All of these positive changes came out of his year of therapy. With his therapist's help, he had developed the ability to analyze his responses and understand the events that precipitated his rages. In addition, he developed lifelong skills to deal with emotional challenges.

During the year or so that the therapeutic process is unfolding, the child is still struggling with their anxiety and/or depression. In fact, they may even get more anxious or depressed while they build trust with a new person and start to examine the issues that make them feel depressed and anxious. Part of my job is to support the parents and reassure them that this is how the process of therapy works, to reassure them that things will get better.

I explain to parents the importance of the connection and establishment of the foundation. I also explain what is happening with their child's brain. Brains change through experience. The experience the child is having with the therapist creates changes in the brain on the cellular level, which eventually translates to changes in behavior. That neurological change takes time and repetition. When the brain is challenged through the therapeutic process, neurons create new connections with other neurons.

When I see children for follow-up visits, I have what may seem to an onlooker like a casual conversation; however, I am looking for patterns of thinking and problem-solving that are different than the time before. When I start to see the child struggling to think through a question, then I know that the process of changing pathways has begun in their brains. I do not need to hear a right answer; I want to hear and see a child's struggle to choose the answer that feels right to them. Eventually the new healthy way of connecting becomes the preferred pathway in the brain; this is when changes in behavior become more obvious.

Parents often feel at a loss for what happens behind the closed doors of the therapist's office. To make it even more confusing, most sessions for tweens consist of about seventy-five percent play and twenty-five percent talking. Many children report to their parents that the therapist was nice, but parents often worry that little will come out of the therapist talking to their child about the family pet or playing games. The relationship between therapist and child is the leading factor that helps heal a child. Parents can not only learn what the therapist is doing, they can acquire the skills that work to heal their child and support the therapist's work at home. It is a matter of learning a new set of skills.

When the child learns to cope with a difficult emotion or devise a plan for handling a troubling situation, the brain lays down a pathway from one part of the brain to another using neurons. As a result, when the child encounters similar personal challenges in the future, their brain already has a healthy blueprint for handling the situation. The relationship between the therapist and child creates a strong experience of an emotional connection which sets the stage for healing to occur in the brain.

In each session, the therapist deliberately shapes the child's brain and helps them to make healthy, strong connections. When the child feels like their therapist is interested in them and they listen and understand them, or at least try to understand them, breakthroughs happen. When children have fun with their therapist and experience the positive feelings of being appreciated and admired, healing is not far behind. A good therapist also empathizes and knows how to be with the child when they enter into their dark places. When a child is afraid, the therapist is right alongside them mirroring their feelings and validating their experience. The therapist does not judge their feelings, which makes the child feel accepted. When a child feels accepted, rather than judged, they will feel more comfortable showing other feelings too.

If they keep their feelings inside, these feelings will multiply and create insecurity, which leads to feeling more anxious and withdrawn. If someone likes them, cares about them, and wants to understand them, they are more likely to let uncertainties, anxieties, fears, and depression all come out in the safe place created by the therapist. The therapist can help them make sense of it and to put it into perspective, and teach them coping skills to ease their pain.

By teaching a child to resolve their feelings, a child learns how to handle their feelings in an effective way, to not be afraid of feelings, and how to deal with them. The goal is not to get rid of the feelings, but to not react to them with behaviors that are disruptive or out of control. If a child feels sad and overwhelmed that their grandparent died, they can learn to express all those feelings through talking and crying, instead of throwing an angry tantrum, which is a mask for unresolved grief.

Miguel was seven years old when his grandmother died. She battled cancer for several months and then entered hospice care during the last three months of her life. Miguel was so close to her that he referred to his grandmother as "Mom." I first saw him a few weeks after his grandmother had passed, after he began misbehaving at school, and refusing to follow directions at home. During our play therapy sessions, he would build elaborate houses out of Legos with landscaping, vehicles, and people. He would then take a large T. rex and have it stomp around the floor and destroy his beautiful creations. He did this many times. As he was building his house, I would comment at the details and how comfortable it looked. He did not say much in return. Occasionally he would nod.

When the T. rex stomped about, I got a little more animated

and exclaimed, "Oh my, he is destroying everything! Watch out!" Miguel smiled and stomped the T. rex harder.

One day after the carnage, I said, "That T. rex sure is mad."

Miguel said, "No, he's not mad."

I replied, "Oh? He looks mad to me because he's destroying everything. What is he?"

Miguel stopped stomping his dinosaur, sat back on his heels, and said, "He's sad."

I agreed with him, "Oh, yes, that makes sense to me. He is so very sad. He just wants to break everything he is so sad."

Tears welled up in Miguel's eyes as he nodded.

"Do you think there's something else to do when T. rex feels sad instead of breaking things?" I asked.

He looked at me and said, "Yes, let's build another house."

We built another house together and this time the T. rex just looked at the house. We eventually continued playing with the dinosaur, but the destructive storyline played itself out. He played with the people in the house, showing daily routines of his parents making dinner, children playing and doing homework, the family watching television, and the parents putting the children to bed. His behavior also began to shift at home and at school. After more play therapy sessions over a few months of time, he learned to appropriately express his sadness about missing his grandmother, and get back to the well-behaved child his teachers and parents knew him to be.

Let's take a closer look at what happened in this scenario with Miguel. From the outside it would appear that Miguel and I, as his therapist, were simply playing, but there were many factors that facilitated this young boy's healing. Therapists employ therapeutic tools that are highly effective in getting positive results, especially for children who struggle with anxiety and depression.

Often parents imagine treatment for anxiety and depression for their children resembling the process of taking a sick animal to the vet. When you bring your animal to the vet, you lay your pet on the table and stand back as the vet does their magic. They touch your animal and look at their eyes and ears as you passively stand by.

After some time, they say something like, "Okay, we need to run some tests on Fido."

The vet then emerges half an hour later and gives you a prescription. This is often parents' expectation when bringing their children in for treatment.

Gathering information from a child is different than gathering information from an adult. Our expectation from adults is that they will tell their provider what they want, what they need, and what is wrong. Children don't do that. They don't offer up this information to their parents and they are even less likely to share with a provider. A psychiatrist can certainly get information from interacting with and observing the child; however, she gathers most information by analyzing as the child, parents, and psychiatrist sit in the room together and exchange needs.

Children need to have their emotions balanced, to be nurtured, to be understood, to feel safe, and to feel validated. The parents need to be able to nurture and discipline their child effectively. They need to feel respected and they need information about how to help their child. It's helpful to imagine yourself as one of the legs of a healing tripod. All three legs are necessary to support the treatment goals. Without any one of the legs, the tripod topples over.

A mother and a father brought their twelve-year-old son for an evaluation. Their son was withdrawn, isolating himself and not talking much. He was shut down and behaving irritably with his family.

The parents said, "Our son is withdrawn and depressed, and we don't know what to do."

When I spoke with the family, they were reluctant to disclose the details of their problems. Much of the information they provided was vague. I felt like they had concerns about their experience with their child that they weren't telling me. Their son was experimenting with smoking marijuana. Their main goal of treatment seemed to be to get their son to stop smoking marijuana. One of my intentions in that meeting was to understand the family dynamic and the child's struggles. His smoking marijuana was just one of many factors I was considering. This boy was significantly anxious and depressed and he wanted to feel better. We had three different agendas in the room. It took many meetings; we sometimes met twice a week. It took at least a month to get all of us on the same page and get the strong tripod set. Once we got the tripod set and the parents understood that there was more to it than cannabis use, we started to make progress. Their son was trying to alleviate his moods, especially his anxiety. When we understood all the concerns, we were able to formulate a hierarchy of treatment goals.

We started him on medication to treat his anxiety and depression. We got him into group therapy to target his anxiety, to help him learn coping mechanisms, and to decrease his social anxiety. We also got him into a family therapy process to strengthen the family's ability to communicate their needs and concerns in a way that was more validating and helpful to the parents and their child. Rather than just telling him to stop smoking pot, the parents started to focus on what his specific needs were, like his need for more nurturance, validation, and time spent with his parents. He also needed to be guided in social skill development. He needed tutoring, as school was a big source of his anxiety. Once we were able to understand everyone's needs, it was smooth sailing.

We started out off-balance because we had different needs. What it took to get us in balance was for each of us to appreciate the other's needs. I first need to understand the child's needs, then help the child get to know both his parents' needs and my needs. Most children realize that I care. To the best of their ability, they usually give me all the information I require. Helping parents understand my needs and the child's needs sometimes can be challenging because adults have more psychological defenses. They tend to be more guarded.

The critical information that I want to know from parents is sometimes the last thing they feel comfortable telling me; they often only share it after I gently, but persistently, persuade them. I need to know their deepest fear about their child.

During med school an instructor taught us how to give a physical examination to a patient.

The instructor said, "If you just listen to your patients, they will always tell you what's wrong."

I firmly believe that. I believe that if parents can talk with their psychiatrist, and the psychiatrist can listen, the parents will always share what's wrong. It's usually the one thing they don't want to say. It's the thing they feel fearful or shameful about saying, which can make all the difference for their child. That one factor is often just the thing I want to know. That's where the focus of treatment needs to be.

The fear these parents had about their twelve-year-old was that he was contemplating suicide. It took a while for them to trust me enough to share that with me.

They started by saying, "My son is using marijuana. We really want him to stop using drugs."

They avoided their big fear while in the room. They told me that their son's use of marijuana was making him apathetic, causing him to isolate himself and affecting his judgment. Then they shared that were afraid he was hanging out with the wrong kids. They told me how sad they were about the distance created by their son withdrawing from them.

Finally, they admitted that they were afraid he would withdraw so much that he would become suicidal, and they wouldn't know how to save him. Now we were getting to the heart of the issue. With this vital information we could formulate a treatment plan to target the danger of suicide. This treatment plan included addressing the marijuana use, and also treating the critical problem of his risk of suicidal behavior.

It's common for parents to second-guess their gut feelings. This comes from the fear of losing their child, the most extreme example of which is for a child to commit suicide. It's beyond scary to imagine. It's frightening to face the prospect that your child may take his life when you have spent your life trying to make his life better. This inner conflict plagues many parents and creates a denial of the risk of suicide. Parents' natural defense against a conflict that seems too unspeakable and unthinkable is to not think about it, which leads to denial. I don't think that parents purposely try to keep information from the psychiatrist or therapist. Often, it's just part of their defense mechanism to deny their gut feeling. However, it is essential that parents push through their reluctance, speak up, and share their deepest fear if they want to help their child. It's the psychiatrist's (and therapist's) job to create a rapport and a safe space that allows parents to be more vulnerable and begin to express those deep fears.

Parents need to give as much information as they remember about their child's development, starting in infancy, in order to support their healing process. Parents are often surprised to hear that we need to gather history so far back, but it does impact their behavior today. When I think about a child and their psychiatric needs, I want a good overview of who they are and how their personality developed. Information about what they are like when they're not depressed or anxious. I am interested in what their personality baseline is like. I want to know what it is like for parents when they are interacting with their depressed or anxious child. I want to know what the parents are feeling.

PREGNANCY

Was it difficult? Premature? Easy? Was it a planned or unexpected pregnancy? I discuss with parents the details of their feelings about the pregnancy, what the birth was like, and if there were any complications during the birth process. It's important to know if the child spent any time in the neonatal ICU versus being able to go home with the parents right away. I also ask parents what it was like in those first couple of months for the parents and the child. What was the bonding and attachment like? Was the child colicky or easy? Knowing the feelings of the parents during that zero-to-three-months timeframe is essential. I want to know if there were any conflicts in the home. Also, if parents were having any particular concerns about their child at that young age. I want to hear about it. Were they concerned that their child was not making eye contact? Were they concerned that their child was behaving in an unexpected way? I want to know if, in the child's early years, the parents were gone from the home (i.e. for illness or deployment), as this can affect issues with anxiety. It's important to know if there was any trauma, not just physical or sexual abuse, but also the trauma of injury—did they fall or hit their head or was anybody rough with them? The reason I want to know all of this is because I want to understand what the foundation of the relationship is between the child and parents. I want to analyze if the foundation of the relationship is secure or insecure, or if there's any place where anxiety or depression might have had a place to start.

Many parents are surprised to learn that factors from a past time might have an effect today and can be tempted to give me the blanket statement that everything was fine. I will often have to ask more detailed questions to help create a complete picture. I want to know about the joy experienced during that time. I also want to know about the fears felt by parents and children because fears lead to the development of psychological defense mechanisms.

When psychological defense mechanisms are created in a parent, the parent behaves in certain ways with their child, to which the child reacts. If parents fear that their child has autism, and that they won't be able to handle it, that fear creates in the parents defense mechanisms like denial and avoidance. Parents can unknowingly deny that there are issues or developmental struggles with their child and as a result not take the child to see the pediatrician, developmental neurologist, or psychiatrist. This can delay the child from receiving appropriate and timely treatment for their struggles.

The avoidance might also be that the caregiver begins to avoid the child, which can have devastating consequences by creating distance between the caregiver and the child. The opposite can also happen where the parent becomes so overly close and protective of the child that the child cannot develop their own sense of personal boundaries. How parents and babies interact sets up a trajectory for how the parent-child relationship will develop throughout the child's life.

Knowing the details of the origins of the parent and child relationship gives me clues about where and how to address the dynamic and facilitate healing experiences for parents and their child. Individual and family therapies can target resolving early attachment and bonding issues to help pave the way for healing.

It's best to think of the process of therapy as a long-term proposition rather than a series of short-term solutions to situational issues. The goal of therapy is to facilitate cognitive, emotional, psychological, and spiritual development in your child, so that your child can learn to make decisions for themselves that are aligned with their self-realization. We've talked about relationship-building as the foundation to promoting the healing process. The process of therapy is designed to help the child learn how to build healthy relationships with the therapist and his or her parents.

The Healer Parent is able to take this long view of therapy. They learn how to ask questions that enhance their child's ability to build healthy relationships.

The Healer Parent's statements, questions, and expressions of concern to the therapist sound more like these: "We have been working together this week to understand how to meet the demands of fifth grade. One of the issues we're struggling with is completing homework and turning it into the teacher. How can I help my child develop good study habits and ease up the struggle of doing homework each night?"

It's the same question asked by the Fix-It Parent, but it comes as a question with a goal to work together toward, rather than from the perspective of their child having a problem that needs to be solved.

Instead of focusing exclusively on completion of tasks, the Healer Parent asks the therapist for help with the process of completing the task. Those kinds of questions and statements also allude to the idea that there might be some anxiety or depression, or other spiritual or emotional conflict that may be an obstacle for the child and or the parent to complete the task.

When a Healer Parent asks this kind of question, the therapist is often able to embark on a discussion toward finding a workable plan.

The therapist can say to the parent and the child, "Okay, let's talk about this. Let's talk about what happens when you think about doing homework. What happens to you when you're thinking about homework? What kinds of feelings and thoughts come up for you even before you sit down to do homework?"

That opens the door for a discussion. It brings the parent into the process. It brings the parent into the therapy session. It also brings the child in to discuss and share their experience with not only the therapist, but also their parent. When a parent asks this type of question, the therapist now has an opportunity to model how to validate the struggle and begin a process toward successful change for the child. When these solution-focused questions are asked, the parent can learn from watching the therapist how to interact with their child in a healthy way and take it home.

FOUR WAYS TO PARTNER WITH YOUR THERAPIST

1 Provide information to the therapist from a shared-experience perspective.

Ideally, parents would give information to the therapist that depicts the struggle as an experience shared by both the parents and the child. With this practice, the team moves from identifying the *child* as the patient to identifying the child's *struggles* as the family's struggles (hence, the word "shared"). Parents can begin to shift into this mindset by using more "we" statements instead of "him" or "her" or "my child."

For example, "We are struggling with communication. We are struggling with getting chores done. We are struggling with feeling distant from each other. We are struggling with managing our irritability and frustration."

When parents frame their struggles in the "we" format, it automatically puts the therapist in a position to help improve the dynamic between the parents and the child, to see them as a whole entity. Therapists are trained in individual therapy, couples therapy, and family dynamic therapy. When parents realize that therapists have this training, and this way of looking at the family unit, they can capitalize on the therapist's training and draw out insights and wisdom from the therapist. When parents present their problems as a shared concern, they demonstrate that they want treatment addressed in a way that includes them too.

If a parent comes in identifying the child as the patient, this may unknowingly put the therapeutic work in the framework of simply working with the child on an individual basis.

When the parent comes in saying, "*We* have this issue we want to work through," this statement optimizes the therapist's family dynamic training and the focus of therapy shifts into viewing the issue as a family issue.

No child exists outside of their primary caregiver system, the family dynamics–focused therapy can be helpful, and ultimately healing.

2 Get information from the therapist.

If the parent asks the child during the drive home what they talked about in therapy, most children will say some version of, "I don't know."

Parents will then attempt to get a clearer answer by asking things like, "What did you discuss exactly?"

Most of the time, the child is simply not able to answer. The space a child shared with the therapist is a special space where they are free to feel vulnerable. As they leave the therapist's office they may still be feeling sensitive, but without the same safety and security of the therapist's office. The child may not remember details to tell the parent. The child may also be feeling defensive and irritable; these feelings are normal as they transition from the therapy space to their regular life space.

Parents need to ask the therapist before they leave the office, "Can I please have the last five minutes of the session so that we can do a recap of the therapy?"

That's the best opportunity for the parent to ask the therapist, "Why is my child struggling? What can I do to help resolve the struggle?"

Many therapists won't readily offer this, so parents need to be proactive and ask.

3 Stay in the waiting room during the session.

I always recommend when I do therapy that parents stay in the waiting room so that I may call upon them at any time during the therapy session. When a parent remains in the waiting room, the child gets the sense that the parent is interested and is sharing the experience with them. This simple act goes a long way to help with bonding and trust-building between parent and child. I can't underscore enough how disappointing it is for a child when they leave the therapy session to go to the waiting room and have to wait for their parent to return. It's disheartening. I see their faces and body slump down when they walk into an empty room. Besides being available to greet your child at the end of the session, your presence may be needed during the session. There often are times when I've been doing therapy with young children that they want to leave in the middle of the session and share something with their parent or bring them in for just two minutes to share an experience. It's important that parents are there, as this is a tangible experience for the child that their parent is available during times of need.

4 Confirm the next appointment in front of your child.

It's helpful for children to hear their parents confirm with the therapist the next appointment time and date, even if therapy occurs at the same time and day each week. Confirming availability is never a redundant exercise. It reinforces the expectation of stability. It shows the child that the parent is reliable, the therapist is reliable, and they are both interested in making sure that this safe place is available for them. It's an unconscious process that builds trust and security for the child.

> This entire partnering process between the parents and therapists sets the stage for healing to continue at home. The steps of the process include:
>
> 1–parents bringing a child to therapy,
> 2–meeting with the therapist for a few minutes at the beginning to discuss the common struggles and goals,
> 3–getting information from the therapist and giving information to the therapist,
> 4–meeting and then staying while the child is in therapy,
> 5–coming in to the therapist office upon conclusion,
> 6–highlighting the importance of that time together,
> 7–making a plan for the next week.

All of these steps are part of the process to form a healthy partnership. This example of partnership allows for each individual to be acknowledged and valued, and for the common struggle to be valued and addressed. This effort will not be lost on your child. For a child in a family to have this example, of even just one hour of working together per week, makes a lasting impression both psychologically and neurologically. When the relationship is healthy, the brain begins to lay down the pathway of knowing what a healthy partnership is. This sets up a lifelong paradigm for the child's brain to utilize so that whenever they approach any new relationship or situation, their brain has a blueprint for what a healthy interaction should be, and how to do it. This kind of connection supports healthy development and lifelong success in all arenas: spiritual, physical, mental, emotional, and psychological development and well-being.

When the tools and techniques of the Healer Parent are used, you naturally form a healthy partnership with your child. When parents can partner with their child, their prognosis for healing is strong. A family's level of ability to partner is evident within the first few moments of my meeting the family.

I completed an intake on a twelve-year-old girl who had been suffering from depression for many years. One year prior to her appointment with me, her depression took a turn for the worse and she started to have suicidal ideations. She did not tell her parents about her suicidal ideations until five days before they came to see me. When she told both of her parents about her wishes to die, both parents cleared their schedules in order to attend the appointment with their child.

When they arrived for their first appointment, I took the three family members back into my office and they all squeezed in to sit on my couch, which is rare. Generally, when I am working with two parents and a child, two people sit on the couch and one person sits on the chair. This family, however, chose to all sit together on a couch that's just a little bigger than a love seat. They seemed comfortable sitting close to each other. In this case, Dad sat closest to me, with Mom next to him and the daughter at the end of the couch. When I interviewed the family, I included all three, but I directed my questions to the child. During that period the parents listened attentively while I conversed with their child. She confidently engaged in conversation with me and described her feelings and her experiences.

Much of the information she shared with me, her parents heard for the first time. They did not realize how long or how intensely their daughter had been suffering with depression and suicidal ideations. This girl was a highly accomplished, straight-A student, and an athlete with an active social life. Unlike many children struggling with depression, she participated in her family. Her parents noticed that over the previous year she had gotten more irritable with her younger siblings, but she hadn't completely withdrawn from the family.

I was able to do 90 percent of my interview by conversing directly with the child as her parents offered emotional support. After my interview with the child, I spoke with her parents, and they did not repeat any of the information the child shared with me, rather they offered their unique narrative which included their experience and their concerns about their child. They did this without being redundant or having to make sure that I heard this same information the child had already given me. They explained how frightened they were about their child having suicidal ideations.

Their main concerns and questions included, "What do we do? How do we help our child? What is the process of treatment?"

In this case, the patient was not the identified patient. Her mother and multiple family members on both sides of the family suffered from depression. This girl had a strong genetic vulnerability for developing a clinical depression. On top of that, she had the perfect storm for getting suicidal ideations: One year prior to them seeing me, her best friend moved away. She had a number of concussions which led to her not being able to play the sport she loved. The concussions also caused a brain injury which took over a year to fully recover from. She developed some stuttering and slow speech. She faced a constellation of major changes…on top of her depression. Happily, she didn't do anything to hurt herself or do any self-harming behaviors. I attribute this to the fact that she came from a very supportive and loving family.

Partnership came naturally for the four of us, largely because this family already knew how to get on the same page with each other. It was easy for me to come in and partner with the family. They readily connected with me, and I felt confident that they could partner well with their child to facilitate her healing. Forming a balanced treatment tripod was easy for us, because this family already knew how to work together and easily integrated a helpful outsider like me.

Partnering with the child happens when the parents and child see each other as individual entities working together to create a relationship dynamic with common goals. When this family first walked into my office, I watched them as they choose their seats. It was clear they all wanted to sit together *because* they function as one unit. When all three of them made room for each other on the couch, this illustrated to me that their unstated intention was to be on the same side of the issue. It showed me how together they are in the process. The child was not struggling alone, her parents were right there with her.

By contrast, when many families enter my office, usually the child sits on one side of the couch closest to me, one parent takes a seat on the opposite end of the couch and does not make room for the other parent, then the other parent looks around my office and sits in the chair next to the door. This is an immediate demonstration of non-partnership. When that happens, I often get three different stories about their concerns. The child usually remains quiet while their parents are in the room. The parents take up most of the time describing their concerns. In addition, Mom and Dad often have different concerns, or one parent will defer to the other parent. Usually the parent sitting in the chair will defer to the parent sitting on the couch. Only when the parents leave the room will the child give me a complete narrative of their experience and concerns. Though it seems daunting, even these families who struggle with partnership can learn to work well together. They simply need some guidance, support, and knowledge of the basics about how to partner with others on the treatment team.

CHAPTER 8

The Ten Tools of the Trade

THE TEN TOOLS OF THE TRADE
FOR BUILDING HEALTHY RELATIONSHIPS

1 Be Fully Present

2 Create Predictability

3 Validate Feelings

4 Practice Acceptance

5 Appreciate Your Child

6 Listen Actively

7 Be Patient

8 Share Clear Agreements and Expectations

9 Become Non-Reactionary

10 Have Fun

1 BE FULLY PRESENT

How the therapist does it:

Of all the tricks of the trade, this one is the most important and incorporates the other tools also. The therapist is gracious, actively listens, and goes out of her way to make each encounter comfortable. She will close the blinds if the light strikes your face; she will adjust the temperature of the room; she will make sure the room is clean and well lit; she will be open and empathetic. She smiles, and speaks gently, making eye contact. Her desk is clear of food and other tasks. Her phone is turned off. She devotes her entire attention and energy to be available to you and your child. With a strong foundation for a strong relationship, the healing happens naturally and with greater ease.

How parents can do it:

When children and their parents interact, they each bring their share of accumulated stressful experiences, worries, thoughts, and feelings from the day, the week, or the month. When parents learn how to put these stressors aside and just focus on their child, they are much more effective at connecting and therefore healing their child. The connection with another person can be likened to a freeway going from one person to the other. During rush hour, many cars clog the freeway and a trip that normally takes thirty minutes with no traffic can take two hours. Likewise, when the energetic freeway is clogged, communication can be slow, nonexistent, or even painful. When parents learn how to clear all their internal cars off the road, then the path of communication is faster and easier.

Alice and her ten-year-old daughter sat on opposite ends of my couch, and even with the simplest of questions like "how was your day?" they quickly escalated into an argument. Alice related that it seemed like all their conversations were difficult and led to frustration and discontent. Their early encounters in my office often left one or both crying. Clearly, they were not making a healthy connection.

I spoke with Alice alone, and asked her what she felt when her daughter approached her. She immediately gave me a list of stresses in her life: some tension with her husband, financial pressure, increased expectations at work, and demands by her other children. In addition, she was worried about her mother's health. Her connection freeway was clearly jammed by other stressors. Alice approached every interaction with overwhelming tension. Her ability to hear her daughter was compromised by her own stress. All she could do was react to her daughter, which didn't allow her daughter to have her own space for her feelings. I asked Alice to start seeing her own therapist so that she had a place to discuss her stressors and develop coping mechanisms to handle her feeling of being overwhelmed. When she learned how to take some of those cars off her freeway, she found that she could listen more to her daughter, and her daughter responded by becoming more communicative and less argumentative.

Parents also benefit from clearing the way. When they can be fully present, they reap the rewards of making a strong and deeply satisfying connection with their child. They can learn and know what is going on with their child. Parents get frustrated and disappointed when they feel like they are not connecting. They genuinely want to understand their child's feelings and needs, and it feels disappointing when they cannot make a connection. Learning to become fully present feels satisfying and helps to heal your child.

2 CREATE PREDICTABILITY

How the therapist does it:

It is even more important to use these therapeutic tricks of the trade when your child struggles with depression and anxiety, because the illness itself has cycles. You cannot always predict when they will have a depressive or anxious episode. There is so much uncertainty inside your child, that to have uncertainty outside of them is very difficult to handle.

Monks, priests, and other clergy live by an extensive set of guidelines and rules. Therapists are also guided by a set of rules for how they behave with their client. When theses spiritual leaders follow those rules, it makes it easier for them to connect to their higher power. When therapists follow the rules, it makes it easier for them to connect to their patients. We can take this concept and use it when we are learning how to connect with another human being, particularly your child. In the therapist's office, the chair, the couch, the rug all remain in the same place, as do the office decorations. Their offices are not stimulating, but comfortable and warm. Like the surroundings they create, therapists are consistent and reliable. They make an appointment and stick to it.

If your appointment is 11:00 a.m., they see you at 11:00 a.m. A good therapist has firm boundaries, and the typical session lasts for fifty minutes.

How parents can do it:

Creating predictability is necessary for parents to practice at home, especially for a child with mental illness. Being predictable is merely doing what you say you are going to do, creating a routine and sticking to it, and maintaining a safe home. For example, in the morning when you take your child to school or give them their breakfast, you can use that time to set the schedule for the day. "After school, I will pick you up, and we can go to the park. After that, I would like you to do your homework while I make dinner. Later, we can do something fun together as a family. Before bed, you may chose a book for us to read together." Setting up a simple routine and sharing it with your child each day may seems redundant, and over-simplified; however, the predictability of the routine reinforces a sense of safety and security.

3 VALIDATE FEELINGS

How the therapist does it:

The therapist understands that acknowledging feelings equates to verbalizing empathy to the child. The therapist will make tentative attempts at identifying the child's feeling by starting with a general description and getting more specific, taking the child's direction to get to the correct label. Then the therapist verbalizes the accurate label, and the child agrees with it.

For instance, the therapist will make a comment of how the patient appears to feel: "What do you feel like? It looks to me like you might be mad."

"No, I'm not mad. But I didn't like something my friend did today," answers the patient.

"Oh? Tell me more," requests the therapist.

"My friend told the teacher I did something I didn't do, she did it. It's not fair. I got in trouble for something I didn't do."

"That's frustrating and disappointing. Did it make you feel sad?"

"Yeah, and I don't like it," the child responds.

"I see that. Please tell me more."

This reflection allows the child to engage in further conversation about the incident and their feelings.

How parents can do it:

Parents can take the same approach as the therapist, and gently ask for clarification. You know your child best, and have the advantage of knowing the subtle signs of your child's feelings. Take an observer stance, and reflect to your child what you see. "It looks like that situation made you feel sad." If you see your child's face soften, or eyes tear up, you know you are on the right track. At this point, you can make an empathetic statement, like "it's hard to be sad," and move closer to your child so that he can lean into you, or extend your arm to place it around his shoulders. Be gentle and slow, and pay attention to how he responds. If he is accepting, move a little closer. If he tenses, back off a little, but not completely. Try to refrain from getting all the details, trying to fix the situation, or offering advice. Instead, stay in that feeling of sadness, and share it with your child. This staying action gives your child the experience of tolerating an uncomfortable feeling until it passes. This is a critical process for children to experience, as it gives them a powerful message of how resilient they are; even in the face of feeling intense feelings, crying, or feeling angry, they can accept support and be okay after a few moments.

4 PRACTICE ACCEPTANCE

How the therapist does it:

No matter what the child says, does, or thinks, the therapist maintains her warm, calm, open, gracious demeanor. The child comes to expect that no matter what happens, that therapist will receive her with the same accepting demeanor each and every time. The child comes to understand that they can bring anything they have going on in that moment or something that happened during the week and know that the therapist can tolerate it all. If a child is sullen, or angry, or rude, the therapist still responds with graciousness. When the child feels happy, joyful, playful, and easy to interact with, the therapist is still accepting. The therapist demonstrates acceptance by allowing all experiences and all feelings. The therapist is a constant and accepting figure. The child can feel free to bring any experience into the session.

How parents can do it:

Practice being gracious with your child. Imagine that you are a hostess, and you want your guests to feel welcomed and comfortable in your home. How do you behave? How do you speak? What do you think while you interact with your guests? Most favored hostesses behave graciously with their guests. They greet their guests with a smile and words of welcome. They offer their guests a drink and appetizers. The hostess engages in conversation about topics of interest to her guests. In all that the hostess does, feels, and thinks, she wants her guests to enjoy their time in her home. Likewise, do the same for your child. Approach your child with words of welcome. Offer them something to eat and drink. Partake in whatever your child wants to do: play a game, read a book, do crafts, or just sit together talking about topics of interest to your child. Most importantly, commit to the intention of accepting your child with love and understanding. This acceptance will allow your child the freedom to share anything about themselves.

5 APPRECIATE YOUR CHILD

How the therapist does it:

Appreciating a child offers them a sense of value. That value comes from people that they love and that are the most influential in their lives. Appreciation includes a combination of both gratitude and compliments. An effective therapist feels grateful for the opportunity to facilitate healing for a child and his family. This is an internal process that is sometimes verbalized to the child. I tell my patients each time we meet how glad I am to see them, and note something unique about them. For instance, I care for an eleven-year-old boy who likes to organize my toy box. I make a point of asking him if he'd like to do some organizing; I then share with him how much I like that he does that for me. I also follow it up with a statement like "those organizational skills are going to be very helpful in whatever you choose to do in the future. It's a really cool thing about you!" Incidentally, it's also a product of his autism spectrum disorder and obsessive compulsive disorder. We work hard to find the right balance between capitalizing on symptoms that are helpful and minimizing symptoms that cause struggles.

How parents can do it:

Trade general compliments for specific compliments. General compliments, like "you are great," are not deeply felt by the child. Specific compliments help a child feel valuable, noticed, and special for their unique qualities. If a child presents you with a picture they made, a general compliment would be, "That's a nice picture, thank you." A specific compliment requires that we take the time to pick up the picture with two hands, look at it, and take a few moments to take it in. Make sure your facial expression shows interest and you look pleased. Then make eye contact with your child and share specifically what it is you like about the picture, and be honest. A child will pick up on your true feelings. If you like the way they colored in the lines, or the way they colored out of the lines, share that with them.

Express exuberance: "I love how you use pink right here. I love how you made the eyes so dark." Take time to notice the details and give your sincere and complimentary opinion.

Don't criticize or offer suggestions, like "maybe next time you should try coloring in the lines," or "oh, it seems like it's only half done." Don't make any judgmental or critical comments.

Appreciating something your child has done helps your child feel better about themselves. There is another, deeper level of appreciation which involves offering a compliment about who they are. If you notice that your child is playing well with a friend, mention that. If the child asks a question that demonstrates their compassion, tell them, "That's so thoughtful of you to think about your friend's problem." Use the words "I like…," to start your appreciation of who they are. "I really like it when you…," "I like how you are so kind," "I like how even though this activity is a challenge, you are trying very hard."

6 LISTEN ACTIVELY

How the therapist does it:

The therapist uses active listening skills to show the child how well they listen and how truly they want to understand the child's experience. Active listening entails listening while reflecting back to the child what the therapist is hearing, and asking questions to understand the child's experience.

How parents can do it:

Most people in this culture listen in a way that they don't clear the road between themselves and another. Make eye contact, sit in a way that is inviting, and lean or get down on the child's level. If the child is on the floor, sit on the floor instead of bending over to talk to your child. Listen more than talk. After you ask a question simply sit, be quiet, and patiently wait. Mirror the facial expressions of the child. Notice when the child is not making eye contact and be ready to offer your eye contact (and a warm smile) as soon as your child looks up. Pay attention to your tone of voice. Think before you speak. If the child has said something or done something that creates irritability or anger inside of you, calm yourself before reacting. The Healer Parent does not allow that reactivity to be translated in their tone of voice when they speak back to the child. If there's a reaction brewing inside of you, take a deep breath before speaking. This is a practical step you can take to help you calm down. Don't spew your feelings; rather, acknowledge your child's feelings. Quickly turn your attention to what your child needs. Reflect back what the child said: "it sounds like your interaction with your friend was upsetting for you. Is that right?" Repeat what they said so your child knows you have heard it.

7 BE PATIENT

How the therapist does it:

After years of training, supervision, and practice, therapists learn to resist the urge to fix their patient's problems, and they learn to tolerate the uncomfortable feeling that arises when someone they care about (their patient or client) struggles. *It is the process of struggling that teaches children how to resolve their conflicted feelings and thoughts, and then change their behaviors. It is the struggle that stimulates and challenges the brain to create new pathways. It is the act of sharing in that struggle that creates closeness between the child and the therapist.* The long-term benefits are profound. In addition to making lasting changes in his brain, he learns that he can tolerate struggling to make changes to better his situation, and he gains confidence and improved self-esteem.

How parents can do it:

It is understandable that you have the urge to jump in and fix things when your child is upset. We want nothing more than for our child to feel better. Also, as adults, we have all kinds of life experience and helpful answers. It's tempting to jump and say "don't do…" and "do…" and solve the problem. That's not how children learn, they have to experience life and learn from it just as we did. While your child is sharing something upsetting with you, note in your mind what is needed, but remain silent until your child finishes. Being patient helps us not lapse into becoming a Fix-It Parent. Listen to the story and help the child unfold their own story before you rush with solutions. The healing intervention is to ask questions, rather than fix things for your child. Help them think through and problem solve to find their own solutions. Help the child understand their experience and what might be happening in a situation. Support their options in terms of behavior, thinking, and actions they might take. Let the child choose the behavior or thought process.

Parents of clients will often ask me, "How do I be patient? My child does need to get to school on time/get their homework done, etc."

You can acknowledge to your child, "I'm feeling really stressed out right now. I'm feeling like we need to hurry to get to school on time. I need for us to take a breath together and figure out what it is that's going on so we can get ready and get to school before the bell rings."

It's beneficial for the parent to be present, accept themselves, and validate their feelings in order to help them be patient with their children. This offers powerful positive modeling for your child. The child can observe that their parent is being kind to themselves and decide, *Maybe I can do that too. I can take a breath like Daddy.*

8 SHARE CLEAR AGREEMENTS AND EXPECTATIONS

How the therapist does it:

They have clear expectations and keep their agreements. A thoughtful therapist will give as much warning as possible and be gracious about having to reschedule. They will let the patient know in very clear terms, "I cannot be with you this Friday; however, I can make an appointment for the following week."

Therapists give options and choices and are clear about what they are able to do and not able to do. They are reliably consistent. They say what they mean and then follow through. They think before they speak or act, and a therapist knows what they intend to convey before they extend a connection or an insight. Every action and each spoken word is thoughtfully carried out with the intention to be therapeutic to the client. The demeanor of a helpful therapist is gracious and unconditional. Sometimes it's hard to be that way as a therapist because we have our own feelings, too. However, it's the therapist's responsibility to check in with their feelings, be honest about what they are feeling, and not let it interfere with the work they are doing with the patient.

How parents can do it:

Parents can learn to make clear agreements and expectations when they understand that their feelings of anger, irritability, or impatience are often generated because they want their child to follow their agenda. For instance, perhaps a parent wants to leave the house within ten minutes and the child does not feel the same urgency. When parents don't manage their impatience, this can interfere with attempts at connecting with their child. Like the therapist, parents can learn to make clear and stated expectations...what the child can expect from them and what they expect from the child.

It's more effective when parents make these expectations during mundane, non-crisis times. For example, "I need you to get to school on time every day." Or "I need you to do your chores without me having to ask you more than once." It's helpful for the child when they know what to expect from their parents: how their parents will behave, what their demeanor will be, that they are going to be there, and that their parents will follow through. For instance, parents can say, "I would rather spend time in conversation instead of nagging you. I expect that you complete the things you are supposed to do the first time I remind you." The child wants to be liked and accepted even when they exhibit bad behavior. Stating clear expectation creates safety when the therapist does it in the office and when the parents do it at home.

9 BECOME NON-REACTIONARY

How the therapist does it:

No matter what a child shares in a session, a helpful therapist does not get excited, angry, or disappointed. The therapist's outward feelings do not change in response to the child's strong emotions. Even when a child brings a big upset, the therapist does not react to their expressed feelings immediately. They may make comments and reflect to name the feeling and question the child about where that feeling is coming from or what happened, but they do it in a way that is nonjudgmental and not inflamed. Their goal is not to agitate the child. The therapist deliberately avoids adding excitability or instigating energy into the dynamic. The therapist stays calm and nonreactive which makes it easier for the child to accept assistance from the therapist and lessen the overwhelming feelings. Once the feelings are diffused, the therapist can lead the child to understand what happened so they can see the options and choices they missed, but which were there in the situation all along. After they acquire an understanding of the process leading to the upset feelings, they know to look for options when in other similar situations.

How parents can do it:

I have observed a common dynamic between parents and their child. It starts when one person expresses him or herself in a heated fashion. Either the child or the parent will start a conversation with a degree of excitability, whether that's happy excitability or angry excitability. The other person then matches or even trumps that excitability. Then the next person trumps the other's excitability and then both find themselves in an escalation of reactivity. This often explodes like a volcano. Like the therapist, the parent can choose to not react. Instead, the parent can, in a softer tone, ask for more information about whatever the child is presenting. When the parent takes the stance of interest, or wanting to understand more than react, the interaction stays steady and healing, not escalating into a win-or-lose situation. From this space of neutrality, a much deeper understanding for both parent and child can be achieved. Though many parents are tempted to try to force their child to calm down, the healthiest intention is to help a child resolve whatever feeling or experience they have in that moment so that the child can calm themselves down.

Children tell me all the time that when they go into a rage they have no idea what they are thinking, feeling, and doing. To intervene at the level of trying to calm the child when they are out of control is a futile process because the child is not connected to their experience in that moment. The more successful route is for parents to keep the area safe and calm, and to simply reach out and offer an opportunity to connect and wait. From that safer place, the child can bring themselves to a more calming state. The best way to create that is to first come from a peaceful, calm, secure place inside of yourself.

Parents frequently ask me, "How do I do that? How do I calm myself down?" Taking deep breaths is a good start. I recommend parents physically take a step back from their child. The temptation is to move toward an upset child but that will often create more upset. Your mantra needs to be *I don't have to fix this, I just want to help my child be grounded and make a connection.* This is not about forcing or pulling a child to follow a command, it's about offering an invitation.

10 HAVE FUN

How the therapist does it:

As I walk to the waiting room at my office, I smile, think about how lucky I am to have the opportunity to care for someone's child, and I acknowledge the feeling of contentment that is generated by that appreciation. This allows me to focus my attention and greet my patient with happiness. Since I take care of children with serious mental illnesses, it's not always an easy encounter, and often we have serious and difficult conversations. We don't have "fun" in the usual sense of the word. We do, however, make a healing connection, and from that connection comes a profound experience of hope that is deeply satisfying. Other therapists who see children every week have their ways of having fun too. During play therapy, therapists play along with the kids, and they allow themselves to enjoy it. During talk therapy, therapists can have an interesting conversation, laugh at a joke, or share an enjoyable experience. When therapists have fun during interactions with children, connections get made.

How parents can do it:

When people have fun they are no longer worried. We are not self-conscious or thinking about all the other tasks we have to do. We are in the moment. When people have fun with another person they are present and connected. That's when you know everything is okay in that moment between the two of you. When a child and their parents share moments of enjoyment it allows for the brain to relax. The psyche and all the senses let go. It allows people to feel vulnerable with each other. When parents are vulnerable they clear the freeway between themselves and their child. Parents gain an understanding of their child's experience and share love. Fun removes the obstacles between you and your child and both of you feel closer.

Many parents complain to me that they feel their child is not having fun anymore. At that point I will often ask them, "Are you having fun anymore?" If the answer is "no," there's an opportunity for Mom or Dad to commit to sharing more moments of fun and giggles with their child. You don't need to book a day at Disneyland, just focus on the small moments that bring more joy and fun (such as going to the park, sharing an ice cream cone, or reading a funny book together). As parents allow themselves to feel joy in an interaction, this feeling will resonate with their child, and the child will have the opportunity to share an enjoyable experience with their parents.

CHAPTER 9

Attunement

Attunement is about taking a slightly different perspective than problem-solving for your children. It includes being interested and caring about your child's experiences, with the added intention of understanding and resonating with your child's feelings, versus focusing solely on the result of your child's behavior.

Eight-year-old Anna sat across from me in silence, with arms folded as her mother described her life before her symptoms of anxiety and depression began.

"She used to enjoy playing with her sister. She was expressive and dramatic, and would often wave her arms wildly when she spoke. Performing for others brought her so much joy. She used to talk to people all the time, make eye contact, and ask a lot of questions."

Mom went on to describe the contrast. "Now, she is irritable and refuses to join the rest of the family when we eat a meal or play a game. She seems to just want to stay in her room. She doesn't even want to play with her friends or go outside."

In my office, Anna responded "no" to everything Mom said. Whenever mom spoke, she threw herself back into her chair, angrily crossed her arms and legs, put on her best pout, and refused to talk. She glared, even when Mom said nice things about her.

"I don't understand; she was doing so well in school and at home. Now she just isn't the same girl anymore," lamented her mom.

Anna is the same girl; however, she had developed depression and anxiety disorders as a result of not being able to manage her intense feelings.

Anna developed anxiety and depression after her mother was diagnosed with a serious illness. Not knowing about her mom's health made her anxious and knowing too much about her mom's health made her anxious. Anna was smart and effective at connecting with people. Mom felt comfortable and shared the details about her health issues with her; but at eight years old, Anna could not handle it. Hearing all the details and the accompanying uncertainty overwhelmed her. She felt scared that she may lose her mother. At the tender age of eight, she did not have the ability to sort out the difference between what might happen, what will happen, and what was unlikely to happen to her mother. She did not have the emotional maturity to tolerate her feelings of sadness, hope, anger, and especially fear.

When a child is confronted by these kinds of overwhelming situations, their psyche develops strategies to cope. Those strategies often include depression, anxiety, or both. The depressed child withdraws from their usual activities and family, and avoids the confusing situation. This child may isolate, brood, become silent, not eat, be lethargic, sleep too much, quit favorite activities, and no longer enjoy her favorite hobbies. The anxious child looks the opposite of a depressed child. The anxious child will look more energized, hyperactive, angry, irritable, silly, intrusive, argumentative, inattentive, and even oppositional and defiant.

In addition to her health challenges, Mom struggled with her own mental health issues. The mom's anxiety made it challenging to deal with Anna. Mom would frequently get frustrated and lose her temper with her daughter. She would try to make statements about her health condition to her daughter to reassure and soothe her fears, but it often had the opposite effect on Anna. Following their conversations, Anna felt even more misunderstood and alone, with strong feelings she was ill-equipped to handle. Mom and Anna were often at odds. Both felt frustrated during their interactions.

Before anyone can help a child calm down, feel better, diffuse an escalating situation, or remedy a crisis, a process called attunement needs to occur. The definition of attunement according to Merriam-Webster's dictionary is "to bring into accord, harmony, or sympathetic relationship; to adjust." This ability to master attunement distinguishes the Fix-It Parent from the Healer Parent.

I spoke to Anna and her mother separately in order to more fully understand their feelings and thoughts. Anna's mom expressed her sadness at the rift in their relationship, and at her helplessness in trying to help Anna feel better about her health crisis. Mom and I discussed how each person's anxiety was clashing with the others. Anna was reacting to Mom's anxiety by feeling even more confused and scared. Once Mom understood this reaction in Anna, she agreed to get therapy for herself in order to resolve her anxiety reactions. Anna also began therapy to learn how to manage her feelings and anxieties when in the presence of her Mom. When both mother and daughter started to learn how to deal with their feelings and express them directly, their interactions became more pleasant, more fun, and more loving.

Anna's mother began to understand that her daughter's young brain could not arrive at an accurate perspective regarding the uncertainty of her illness. Anna's brain simply had not developed the cognitive ability to accurately weigh the risks and probabilities. With the help of their therapist, Mom learned how to adapt her communication style to help Anna handle an extremely stressful family situation. Attunement was required on Anna's mother's part to meet Anna where Anna was at cognitively, instead of expecting Anna to meet her where she was at cognitively.

Attunement is essential in order to effectively meet your child's needs. If you are not in attunement, it feels like whatever effort you make, even though it's sincere and from a place of wanting to be helpful, does not meet your child's needs. This can feel like wasted effort which leads to frustration on both sides. The parent feels ineffective and underappreciated, and the child feels dismissed and misunderstood. It leads to frustration and escalation for both, and an increase in problematic behaviors.

I worked with an eleven-year-old girl, Emma, who was struggling with significant anxiety. Before she saw me, she worked with a therapist for a couple of months. Her therapist suggested that she come to me for an evaluation to see if there was something other than anxiety troubling her and if medication may be necessary. Her parents made the appointment and when I went to the waiting room I saw just the dad in the waiting room.

He said, "My wife is downstairs with my daughter. She refuses to get out of the car. She is too nervous."

After I got the child's medical history from the father, I offered to go downstairs and try to coax her to come to my office. I went down to the car and, sure enough, she was in the back seat with her sweatshirt hood pulled completely over her face.

I said "hello," and waited a few moments.

Then I asked, "Can I just see your face and say 'hi'?"

I saw the hood of her sweatshirt shaking no.

I said, "That's all right. We'll try again another time."

I then spoke to her mother who explained that she was very anxious about meeting new people, and even with her therapist she needed to bring her small dog to feel better about meeting with her.

I explained, "That's fine with me. She's welcome to bring her dog to our appointment next week."

I didn't want to force interaction with her. I wanted to stay attuned to her needs and desires.

The next week, I walked into the waiting room and saw that Emma was there with her dog. She didn't speak very much. Mom was gentle and lovingly coaxed Emma into my office. Once in my office, Mom was present. At the same time, she allowed plenty of time and space for her daughter to just be anxious and to have her experience. She let her daughter converse with me without jumping in and taking over.

Sometimes parents get anxious when their child doesn't answer my questions. In these cases, they often talk over their child, which doesn't give them room to build rapport with me. This kind of taking over or speaking for the child is the opposite of attunement. Emma's mother empathized with her daughter's anxiety, but also allowed for Emma to share her experience, without talking for Emma.

You could feel the attunement between this mother and her daughter. Mom could feel how painful the anxiety was for Emma and understood how to be truly supportive. After we played with the dog for a few minutes, Emma opened up and shared with me about how painful and debilitating her anxiety was. Mom supported her. She did not contradict her daughter's story.

She said, "Yes, I've experienced the same thing with Emma."

I asked Emma's mom my standard question: "What concerns do you still have?"

Mom looked at her daughter and said something like, "I think the anxiety has decreased since beginning treatment."

She then went on to talk about what she has observed, without making assumptions about what that meant for her daughter. Then it becomes a discussion between the three of us, instead of one person talking for Emma.

Mom would essentially say "this is what I see, I'm wondering how you feel about that?" and her daughter was comfortable adding "no, I'm not doing that anymore," or "oh yes, I am still doing that. I am doing those rituals."

Mom protected her daughter's privacy also. Emma was having some anxiety about her clothing. I inquired about this and Emma looked at the mom and then Mom said, "She doesn't really want to talk about the details."

I said, "That's fine, we don't really need to talk about the details. We can just talk about the experience."

This helped the daughter, because the mother maintained her trust with Emma, which is essential to the work we are doing and for preserving the strength of the mother-daughter relationship.

I have seen many other parents who did not understand

attunement. When I would ask their child a question, and the child was reluctant to share the details, these parents fill in the details. Then the trust gets broken between the child and the parent.

The child says, "I don't want to talk about that. Why did you talk about that?" and the child gets more frustrated and annoyed and more shut-down.

Emma never told me what it was about her clothing that she was struggling with, but she continued to tell me about her experience, so I was able to get some clarity about what work we still needed to do. At one point, we were on the fence about increasing medication. Emma didn't want to increase medication; she wanted to work with her therapist to manage her anxiety.

Mom said, "I can support that because we have come a long way."

This was more of a discussion and an acceptance of where Emma was with her needs and desires.

Emma's mom truly understood how much her child was working and how she was feeling, and allowed for her child to develop her own goals for managing her anxiety. Emma made a major improvement over the six weeks we worked together. Her anxiety went from debilitating to the point where she couldn't leave the car, to walking into my office looking completely relaxed while she giggled and talked with me about her feelings and concerns. All this improvement in just six weeks! Emma even looked forward to plans for the summer to help out at her church camp where she would interact with strangers. She couldn't begin to think about showing her face to strangers when I first met her. I believe that Emma recovered quickly because her parents were attuned with her. This attunement allowed the medication to work quickly, it allowed for Emma to drop her guard and feel understood and supported. She didn't feel any pressure to be anything other than who she was. She was accepted for where she was with her anxiety.

Attunement is basically being on the same page with the child. It's the parent seeking to understand the child's needs, feelings, and wants in a moment, then meeting those needs, feelings, and wants. It's a three-step process. It's gathering information and then taking action.

STEP ONE: <u>Gather information</u>

The first part of establishing attunement involves gathering information from your child about what they want, what they need, and how they're feeling in the moment. Observe their behavior and their expression.

Ask them, "How are you feeling?" or "What do you want?"

The trick is to ask this in a non-demanding way with no trace of irritation. After you sit down next to your child, be silent and observe. In your stillness, you have the opportunity to feel what your child is feeling, and your child has no reason to escalate to be heard.

Clarify with the child what they just said by asking, "What does that mean?"

If they say "I'm hungry" or "I want my sister to go way," the parents can ask, "What does that mean for right now? Do you want a few minutes alone? Do you want to just sit with me for a few minutes?"

Be sure you understand exactly what it is your child wants or needs.

If the child expresses a feeling, like "I feel angry," explore that by asking questions like "what are you angry about?" or "what can I do to help you with your anger?"

STEP TWO: <u>Acknowledge feelings</u>

If your child is sulking around the house, slamming doors, or withdrawing and being needy and irritable, the way to express validation of those feelings is to simply express it back to them.

You can say, "It seems like this moment is difficult for you. I understand that you are having a hard time, that you feel sad."

Repeat whatever words the child uses to express their feelings. Give them reassurance that the feeling will pass and that you are able to tolerate their transitory upset.

You can simply state, "I know it feels sad right now, I am here with you. I will be with you until it passes."

Acknowledging feelings is one of the most successful ways to connect and stimulate healing for your child.

STEP THREE: <u>Harmonize with your child</u>

This step is about communicating your understanding of your child's experience without trying to change it. Parents can harmonize with their child by asking themselves, *Can I accept that this is happening?* If the answer is yes, you are there. If there is something that you cannot accept, or there is an obstacle to fully accepting your child, then go a step further with some self-inventory or self-exploration. Ask yourself, *Why do my child's feelings make me feel irritable and impatient?* If it is challenging for you to get to a place of harmony and acceptance, you may want to discuss this struggle with your therapist who can provide you with some insight and tools. It is common that a parent's unresolved past issues can be triggered when trying to resolve a difficult situation with their child. An effective therapist can help you work through those unresolved issues, freeing you to be able to harmonize with your child.

It's a huge relief when we feel understood. When children feel understood, they feel connected to their parents, hopeful, and better about themselves. When parents feel effective and confident, everyone feels closer. This closeness helps the child feel more attached to their parent. This attachment alone is healing. When both parent and child are attuned and on the same page, they make huge strides toward healing anxiety and depression.

CHAPTER 10

Stopping Therapy

P arents frequently ask me, after they've been in therapy for anywhere from a few months to over a year, about whether treatment has completed or is not working with the current therapist. If they decide to switch to a new therapist, they want to know how to transition gracefully. It's not an easy decision.

It's essential that the guiding principle for all decisions is what is in the best interest of the child's development and healing process. Oftentimes, a child forms a strong bond with their therapist. That bond is an important element to the success of the therapy; however, there are other elements to the therapy that also need to be effective to warrant staying with a therapist. If the other elements aren't present, it may be time to make a change.

I worked with a ten-year-old girl named Cecily who was diagnosed with an anxiety disorder with some depressive features. Her mother reported significant conflict between her and her daughter, and also between Cecily and her father. Cecily's father never came to treatment. As far as I knew, he was not in individual therapy or couples' therapy with his wife. When they first came to see me, Cecily had been working with her therapist for about eighteen months.

The mom said to me, "I don't know if the therapy is effective. I have seen zero change in my daughter's behavior. She continues to be oppositional and defiant. She continues to argue with her dad and me.

It seems like no relationship in the family is peaceful or cooperative and that has not changed in the eighteen months of therapy."

I asked the mom, "What are you expecting from therapy?"

She answered, "I was hoping my daughter would be less oppositional and defiant and that there would be more peace in the family."

I spoke with the daughter and asked her, "Do you like your therapist?"

She responded, "Yes, I like my therapist."

I asked her, "What do you do in therapy?"

She said, "I don't like to talk very much so we just play games."

That statement raised my yellow flag. Although play is an essential part of therapy with children, it was the fact that Cecily stated that she didn't talk much that got my attention. This little girl loved to talk. Cecily gleefully told me stories and expressed herself clearly. She also argued quite a bit with her mom. She argued with me. Only occasionally would she shut down when emotions ran high or when she felt slighted or hurt.

Given that history, I discussed with the mom and Cecily that, because she was playing and not talking with him, she did not seem to be fully engaged with her therapist. As Cecily did not have her usual demeanor with the therapist, the therapeutic rapport likely had not been established during their eighteen months of working together. That rapport needs to be established within the first few months. I did recommend, in this case, that Mom change therapists. I asked Cecily about how she felt about seeing another therapist, and she said that she felt anxious about changing therapists. She likes her therapist, but was willing to meet a new therapist. I introduced her to a therapist whose demeanor was calm and sweet, but her practice style was more proactive. This therapist establishes rapport and begins the therapeutic work within the first few meetings rather than wait for rapport to be built over the course of eighteen months.

How we handle a transition to a new therapist can make a

significant difference in a child's progress and success. The way we set it up for Cecily was to give her some say.

I told her, "We want you to meet with a new therapist for a couple of sessions. You can decide if you want to continue with her or not. If you like her, great; if you don't like her, you can go back to your old therapist until we find another therapist you like."

She agreed to our plan. I recommended that the mother and daughter go back to the old therapist and tell him that they wanted to try a new therapist. That was anxiety-provoking for the parents and the child because they didn't want to hurt the therapist's feelings. This is understandable because, in therapy, you form a relationship. They returned to the therapist to have one last session and explained that since they had been in therapy for eighteen months and not seen the behavioral changes they had hoped, they wanted to try a new approach. The therapist was quite open and accepting. They had a nice termination session and got to say, goodbye and good luck to each other.

Termination sessions are an important aspect of therapy, whether it is to transition to a new therapist or end a successful treatment. The ending of a treatment process is as important as the beginning and the middle of the therapy treatment period. Just as all satisfying stories have a beginning, middle, and end, so must therapy; for the child, her experience in therapy becomes part of her life story. An abrupt ending to a therapeutic relationship can trigger struggles of abandonment, guilt, and rejection. The child must have an opportunity to say goodbye to an important figure in her life, and to hear from the therapist that there are no hard feelings between them. The child needs the experience of seeing that her therapist feels okay about the child moving on to another therapist and experience. This kind of closure is vital for the child to feel secure in pursuing her goals and moving forward in her life. She needs to move forward without the burden of feeling concerned that she caused harm to another person. The experience of a peaceful and mutually-accepted closure allows for the child to develop the ability to transition smoothly in their future relationships and situations.

Cecily started therapy with the new therapist and did very well. She liked her new therapist. The therapist formed a good alliance with her and was also able to convince Mom to begin her own therapy so she could learn how to decrease her anxiety and stress levels. As a result of this, Mom was able to reduce the amount of anxiety she brought to their interactions. They started to see results within a few months. Part of Cecily's oppositional, defiant behavior included shutting down when she tried to express herself. Cecily learned from her new therapist how to express herself in a way that was not abrasive to the rest of the family. She also learned how to tolerate the healthy levels of conflict that happen in all relationships; she was less likely to shut down during conversations. The new therapist was more effective at meeting the goals identified by the mother and daughter.

It's helpful if parents have a basic understanding of their child's psychological needs, the therapeutic timeline, interactive style, and fit before deciding if it's time to try a new therapist.

Psychological needs

You don't need to understand every one of your child's therapeutic needs, but parents need to have a basic understanding and clarity about what their child needs. When they do, they are better equipped to make healthy decisions. It helps to have a few specific goals for therapy. These goals can be improvement in specific behaviors and generally meeting the needs of the child. One example is that a young child may need to learn how to tolerate frustration so that they can try new activities without having a meltdown whenever they struggle. Another goal might be to help a child understand how to appropriately express to their peers and family their needs for space and time alone, instead of pushing others away or behaving rudely. Also, another achievable goal in therapy is asking the therapist to help a child develop healthier coping mechanisms, so that the child stops cutting themselves.

Therapeutic timeline

Often families engage in therapy without a clear understanding of how long therapy takes or what the timeline should look like. This can result in unnecessary frustration on the part of the parents, the child, and the therapist. Conversely, when everyone understands and embraces the expectations and timeframes of therapy, all parties benefit and are naturally more invested in the process. This mindset benefits the child greatly.

After the rapport building, when the relationship blossoms, the work should begin to show results. Early results can be subtle. You may notice your child is less rude, they spend less time in their rooms, they share more of their accomplishments with you, they make more eye contact, they seem more relaxed, and they interact more. It is helpful for assessing the progress of therapy to check-in with each other about whether expectations are being met. From week to week, share with the therapist the progress you notice along with any concerns that you may have.

Interactive style

The interactive style refers to how kids express themselves in interactions with their parents, their siblings, their teachers, and their peers. Some kids are comfortable expressing themselves and will do so without hesitation. Some children are shy and reserved while others are outgoing and gregarious. Other children are outgoing, but also quite introverted; they are quiet but they still engage. Other children are slow to warm up. They hold back and observe the people around them before they engage in interactions. There are children whose interactive style is to be bubbly and use humor to express themselves. Some children don't use humor. They rely instead on information or fact-sharing to express themselves.

Sometimes kids feel overwhelmed in a discussion because they are anxious. The emotional content becomes overwhelming, or they feel fearful or sad. They may react with more defensive behaviors by becoming oppositional or defiant. They may react physically like lashing out, hitting peers, hurting themselves, or running away. Children who are able to express themselves freely and without much anxiety or excessive defenses don't usually see a psychiatrist or therapist; they are more able to manage their feelings. It's the kids who are unable to regulate their moods, anxiety, thoughts, and behaviors who come to see mental health providers.

One of the reasons to become familiar with your child's interactive style is so you can more accurately assess if rapport is being made with their therapist. If a child is typically open with their feelings, either by expressing verbally or being defiant, I would expect the same behaviors in the therapist's office. They should be able to talk openly with their therapist, and they will learn how to express themselves more effectively.

Parents should feel that their child is comfortable expressing themselves to their therapist. In the case of Cecily, her typical interactive style of enthusiastic talking was not happening between her and her therapist.

Fit

The fit between Cecily and her first therapist was not effective because the therapy was not meeting the goals of the family. The relationship amounted to mostly rapport-building between the therapist and the child, and that rapport never advanced to further therapeutic work together. The fit was not adequate because the therapist was not advancing the treatment approach to meet the goals of the family. Rapport is a part of fit. The therapist has to establish a good rapport, not with just the child but with the caregivers too in order for therapy to be effective.

Along with rapport, fit includes mutual understanding and commitment to working toward achieving the goals of therapy. This means that the parent(s), the child, and the therapist are all on the same page about what to expect and what their work together will be.

Fit is about how the therapist works and how their skill set, perspective, and way of proceeding with the therapeutic process fits with the family's dynamic and tempo. Some families have the ability to tolerate multiple interventions, to accept insights, and then apply them. For these families, the best therapists are going to be those who are proactive and willing to jump in. Other therapists sit back, listen, guide, and gently move families toward change. These are both worthwhile processes. It just depends on the needs of each unique family.

It all comes down to your gut

Ultimately, it's the feeling in your gut that you should trust more than anything else when deciding whether to stay or go. I advise parents that if inside you feel hesitation or trepidation about therapy or the therapist, that needs to be given importance and it needs to be explored, both personally and in therapy. Ideally, when the thought *I don't know if this is right* crops up, clients bring this concern to the therapist and give the therapist a chance to understand and resolve it. If the therapist is open and able to hear your concerns and can enthusiastically engage in a process to resolve the issue—and if your child feels like they are making progress—then stay. That's exactly what therapy is for, working out issues. That's a good fit.

When families step into the office of a mental health professional, they are already in a position of vulnerability. Most people don't seek professional help unless they are desperate for help. This puts them in a vulnerable position right out of the gate and sets up a palpable power differential. It is a therapist's responsibility to diminish this power differential and make all family members feel comfortable and safe. It is the therapist's responsibility to create a sense of safety. Within that safe environment, the family will likely feel comfortable opening up and sharing their vulnerability. Again, this is a gut feeling. If you feel that you can't trust the therapist, believe that you can't be vulnerable, or are holding back, that is something to consider. You owe it to yourself to investigate whether or not there is enough safety created in the therapeutic relationship.

Safety is feeling that you can trust the therapist to lead you through the process of treatment. Safety is knowing that no question is too ridiculous and the health and well-being of your child is honored and protected.

Good therapy and treatment that is effective does come to an end. Honor the process, practice the tools of the trade, and go live a happy, fulfilling life with your children.